LA CUCINA
ITALIANA

ANTIPASTI

PASTA & PIZZA

LA CUCINA ITALIANA

ANTIPASTI

PASTA & PIZZA

Edited by Judith Ferguson

PRION

Published in the United Kingdom 1992 by
PRION,
an imprint of Multimedia Books Limited,
32-34 Gordon House Road, London NW5 1LP

**Editors Judith Ferguson, Linda Osband
Design Terry Allen, Megra Mitchell
Jacket design Megra Mitchell
Production Hugh Allan**

**Original recipes and pictures copyright © NEPI
La Cucina Italiana, Via Mascheroni,
1-20123 Milan
English translation and compilation copyright
© Multimedia Books Limited, 1987, 1992**

British Library Cataloguing-in-Publication Data
Antipasti, pasta and pizza. - (La Cucina Italiana)
I. Ferguson, Judith   II. Series
6541.5945

ISBN 1-85375-029-8

Printed in Italy by New Interlitho

CONTENTS

ANTIPASTI WITH EGGS,

For Italians, the best way to begin a meal is with an *antipasto* ("before the pasta"), a dish designed to prepare the stomach and enhance the main course. *Antipasti* can range from just one item, like a simple asparagus in batter, to a selection of delectable items beautifully arranged on a plate. Essential ingredients loved by Italians — fresh seasonal vegetables, eggs and regional cheeses — form the basis of this important first course. Some *antipasti* dishes can also be substantial snacks.

CHEESE & VEGETABLES

Cheese Dome
Cupola di Formaggio

To serve 6

4 oz/100 g Philadelphia cream cheese

4 oz/100 g Stracchino cheese

4 oz/100 g Robiolina cheese

2 oz/50 g soft Gorgonzola cheese

2 oz/50 g grated Parmesan cheese

6 tablespoons/100 ml very fresh whipping cream

4 slices white bread

Preparation time: about 40 minutes

Remove the cheeses from the refrigerator at least 2 hours before preparation. Finely dice the cheeses and place them all, including the grated Parmesan, in a bowl. Beat and mix to form a smooth, creamy mixture.

Whip the cream and carefully fold into the cheese mixture. Add a pinch of salt and plenty of pepper. Mix well and then place the mixture in the centre of a large, round plate. Mould into a dome shape and decorate it with vertical lines, using a fork.

Cut the slices of bread diagonally into 8 triangles and either toast them or fry them gently in butter until golden brown. Arrange some of the toast or *croûtons* around the cheese dome and serve the rest separately. Garnish as desired and serve.

Ham Rolls
Involtini di Prosciutto

To serve 4

1 small carrot

1 stalk celery

3 oz/80 g Emmental cheese

2 tablespoons mayonnaise

1 teaspoon mustard

8 fairly thick slices lean ham

a little gelatine dissolved in 6 tablespoons/100 ml warm water

1 slice any mild-flavoured cheese

2 stuffed olives

Preparation time: about 40 minutes

Trim and wash the carrot and celery and slice the celery thinly. Cut the carrot and Emmental cheese into thin strips. Place the carrot, celery and Emmental cheese in a bowl and stir in the mayonnaise and mustard. Taste and add salt if necessary.

Spread the slices of ham out on a surface, trimming off any fat. Place a tablespoon of the prepared filling on each slice and fold the ham up into rolls, carefully enclosing the filling. Arrange the rolls on a plate and brush them with a little cool liquid gelatine, making sure that it does not drip. Place in the refrigerator. When the first coating of gelatine has set, remove the rolls from the refrigerator and brush them with another coat of gelatine. Replace in the refrigerator.

Cut the slice of cheese into 8 triangles and the olives into 8 slices.

Decorate each roll with a triangle of cheese and a slice of olive. Garnish as desired and serve.

Augustan Tomatoes
Pomodori Augustei

To serve 6

1 egg

3 very large tomatoes

1 carrot

1 potato

1 slice white bread

butter

4 oz/100 g prawns

2 tablespoons mayonnaise

1 tablespoon mustard

1 tablespoon tomato ketchup

a few young celery leaves

Preparation and cooking time: about 40 minutes

Hard-boil the egg, cool it under running water and shell it. Wash and dry the tomatoes and cut them in half with a sharp knife. Discard the seeds and sprinkle the insides with salt. Place the tomatoes upside-down on kitchen paper and leave to stand.

Trim, wash and dice the carrot and place in a saucepan. Cover with water, add a little salt and bring to the boil. Peel and dice the potato and add it to the carrot once the water has been boiling for 5 minutes. When the vegetables are tender, drain and dry them on kitchen paper.

Finely dice the bread and fry it gently in 1 oz/25 g butter. Finely chop the drained prawns and mix them with the mayonnaise, mustard and tomato ketchup. Blend carefully and then stir in the cooked vegetables and diced bread.

Wipe the insides of the tomatoes with kitchen paper and stand them on a work surface. Stuff them with the prepared filling. Finely crumble the hard-boiled egg yolk and sprinkle it on to the tomatoes. Arrange on a plate, garnish with a few young leaves of celery and serve.

Cheese dome (top), **Augustan tomatoes** (centre) and **ham rolls**

Three-flavoured Pie

Torta ai Tre Gusti

To serve 8

8 oz/250 g puff pastry

2 oz/50 g butter

4 oz/100 g endive, boiled and drained

8 oz/200 g spinach, boiled and drained

1 medium onion

olive oil

½ stock cube

6 oz/175 g very fresh Ricotta cheese

1 thick slice ham, finely chopped

3 eggs

1 oz/25 g grated Parmesan cheese

nutmeg

1 tablespoon breadcrumbs

Preparation and cooking time: about 1 hour plus any defrosting time

Defrost the pastry if necessary. Butter a 10 inch/25 cm pie dish. Finely chop the endive and spinach and put in a bowl. Then finely chop the onion and sauté in 2 tablespoons of butter and the olive oil, taking care not to let it brown. Crumble in the stock cube and keep the pan over the heat until it has dissolved. Then combine the onion with the endive and spinach, mixing thoroughly. Rub the Ricotta through a sieve, letting it fall on to the mixture in the bowl. Then add the ham. Beat the 3 eggs with a pinch of salt and a little freshly ground pepper, the Parmesan cheese and a little grated nutmeg. Pour this into the bowl with the other ingredients. Stir vigorously after the addition of each new ingredient until smooth. Taste and adjust the seasoning.

Preheat the oven to 375°F/190°C/gas mark 5. Roll out the pastry on a lightly floured pastry-board to a thickness of about ⅛ inch/3 mm, then line the pie dish and trim the edges. Prick the pastry with a fork and sprinkle with breadcrumbs. Spread the filling mixture evenly in the dish, then tap the

dish lightly to eliminate air bubbles. Decorate the top with the pastry offcuts and bake for about 30 minutes in the bottom of the oven. Serve piping hot.

Spicy Eggs

Uova Piccante

To serve 4-6

6 very fresh eggs

6 oz/150 g tinned tuna in oil

a handful of parsley

1 oz/25 g capers in oil

1 pickled gherkin

4 anchovy fillets in oil

3 oz/75 g thick mayonnaise

1 tablespoon mustard

Worcestershire sauce

6 stuffed olives

1 head chicory

white wine vinegar

olive oil

Preparation and cooking time: about 40 minutes

Hard-boil the eggs and cool thoroughly under running water. Shell and halve the eggs lengthwise. Remove the yolks and rub them through a sieve into a bowl. Drain the oil from the tuna, purée it and add to the egg yolks. Finely chop the parsley with the capers, gherkin and anchovy fillets and add the mixture to the other ingredients. Mix with the mayonnaise, mustard and a generous dash of Worcestershire sauce to a smooth paste. Taste and adjust the seasoning.

Put the mixture into a piping bag with a round serrated nozzle and fill the 12 egg halves. Arrange on a serving dish. Cut the olives in half and press them into the filling. Place the chicory leaves in the centre of the dish, seasoned simply with salt, pepper, vinegar and olive oil. Serve at once.

Egg Surprise

Sorpresa d'Uova

To serve 4

butter

olive oil

1 small onion, finely sliced

flour

scant ½ pint/250 ml good meat stock

tomato paste

4 eggs

1 thick slice ham

Preparation and cooking time: about 35 minutes

Heat a knob of butter and a tablespoon of olive oil in a small saucepan and lightly fry the onion until transparent. Sprinkle with flour and add the boiling stock in which half a teaspoon of tomato paste has been dissolved. Bring to the boil, stirring constantly. Lower the heat and simmer for 3-4 minutes. Purée and return to the pan. Check and adjust the seasoning to taste.

Hard-boil the eggs, cool under cold running water, shell them and cut them in half lengthwise. Arrange on a plate, curved side up, and coat with the prepared sauce. Garnish each piece of egg with a diamond of ham and serve warm.

Three-flavoured pie (top) and **spicy eggs**

Eggs in Piquant Sauce
Uova Rosate

To serve 6

6 eggs

4 oz/125 g mayonnaise

2 tablespoons mustard

2 tablespoons tomato ketchup

Worcestershire sauce

1 tablespoon/20 ml whipping cream

6 small black olives

2 leaves radicchio, cut into strips

a few sprigs chicory

Preparation and cooking time: about 30 minutes

Hard-boil the eggs, shell them and halve them lengthwise. Sprinkle with salt and pepper. Arrange the eggs curved-side up on a dish, slightly apart from each other. Blend the mayonnaise in a bowl with 2 tablespoons each of mustard and tomato ketchup and a generous splash of Worcestershire sauce. Adjust seasoning to taste. Add a tablespoon of cream.

Pour the sauce over the eggs and sink half an olive into the sauce on the top of each egg. Garnish with radicchio and sprigs of chicory.

Emmental Cheese 'Cake'
Cake all' Emmental

To serve 8-10

4 oz/100 g butter

3 eggs

grated nutmeg

1 teaspoon mustard

1 teaspoon chopped parsley

8 oz/250 g Emmental cheese

8 oz/250 g sliced ham

8 oz/250 g plain flour

1½ teaspoons baking powder

6 tablespoons/100 ml whipping cream

a little butter and flour

Preparation and cooking time: 1½ hours

Pre-heat the oven to 350°F/180°C/gas mark 4. Use butter and eggs at room temperature. Beat the butter until soft and creamy. Mix in the eggs one at a time, beating well to form a smooth paste. Season with a pinch of salt and pepper and plenty of ground nutmeg. Fold in one heaped teaspoon each of mustard and chopped parsley.

Dice the Emmental cheese and the ham, discarding the fat.

Stir the pieces of ham and cheese into the prepared mixture and then add the sifted flour and the baking powder. Mix thoroughly and then stir in the cream.

Pour the mixture into a greased and floured cake tin and bake for about 50 minutes. Before removing from the oven, check that it is cooked by pushing a wooden skewer into the centre. If the skewer comes out clean, the cake is ready.

Allow to cool and then turn out on to a plate. Slice and serve while still warm.

Cheese 'Tear-drops'
Gocce Ovette

To serve 6

1 egg

6 slices fresh white bread

6 slices Pariser cheese

mayonnaise

1 sprig parsley

Preparation time: about 30 minutes

Hard-boil the egg and cool it under cold running water. Using a pastry-cutter, cut 12 tear-drop shapes out of the bread and cheese. Spread each piece of bread with a little mayonnaise and place the pieces of cheese on top, fitting the shapes carefully together.

Shell the egg and chop it coarsely, together with a sprig of parsley. Place a little of this mixture on each 'tear-drop', leaving a border of about ¼ inch/5 mm. Arrange on a tray or plate garnished with parsley and serve.

Eggs in piquant sauce

Eggs Stuffed with Artichokes

Uova Ripiene ai Carciofini

To serve 6

6 large eggs

3 oz/75 g tinned artichoke hearts in oil

2 heaped tablespoons thick mayonnaise

heaped tablespoon mustard

anchovy paste

Worcestershire sauce

1 large slice red pimiento

a few tender chicory leaves

Preparation and cooking time: about 35 minutes

Boil the eggs, which should not have been in the refrigerator. Cool them under running water, shell them and cut them in half lengthwise. Scoop out the yolks and sieve them into a bowl. Reserve the half-whites. Squeeze the oil from the artichokes thoroughly, chop them as finely as possible, then add them to the sieved yolks. Add the mayonnaise, mustard, about 1 inch/2 cm of anchovy paste and a dash of Worcestershire sauce. Mix the ingredients thoroughly, then taste and adjust the seasoning.

Cut out 9 tear shapes from the slice of pimiento with a pastry cutter. Put the prepared mixture in a piping bag with a round, pointed nozzle and fill the 12 egg white halves. Arrange them on a round serving dish. Garnish with the pimiento 'tears' and the chicory leaves and serve immediately.

Lettuce "Cigars"

"Sigari" di Lattuga

To make 24 "cigars"

1 fresh lettuce

5 oz/150 g fresh Ricotta cheese

2 oz/50 g Gorgonzola cheese

1 tablespoon juniper-flavored *grappa* or brandy

dried tarragon

Preparation time: about 25 minutes

Pull out the tender leaves of the heart of the lettuce and wash and dry them gently. Using a sharp knife, remove the central stalks and divide each leaf in half.

Drain and mash the Ricotta and place it in a bowl. Finely dice the Gorgonzola cheese and beat it with the Ricotta to form a smooth, creamy mixture. Stir in the juniper-flavored *grappa,* a pinch of salt and pepper and a generous pinch of dried ground tarragon.

Blend thoroughly and then place a teaspoon of the mixture on each piece of lettuce. Fold up to form cigar-shaped rolls, making sure that the filling does not ooze out.

Arrange the "cigars" around the edge of a plate and garnish the centre as desired. This dish makes an excellent light hors d'oeuvre or can be served with aperitifs.

Italic Cheese Tart

Crostata Italica

To serve 4

8 oz/250 g plain flour

6 oz/150 g butter

3 medium onions

a little butter and flour

1 tablespoon fresh breadcrumbs

8 oz/250 g Italic cheese

3 eggs

¼ pint/150 ml milk

Preparation and cooking time: about 1¼ hours

Sift the flour and a pinch of salt. Cut 4 oz/100 g of the butter into small pieces and rub it into the flour until the mixture resembles fine breadcrumbs. Mix in enough water to make a soft, but not too sticky, dough. Roll the dough into a ball, wrap it in greaseproof paper and place in the refrigerator for 30 minutes.

Meanwhile thinly slice the onions and fry them gently in 1 oz/25 g of butter. Season with a little salt and pepper. If necessary, add a little water to prevent browning. Pre-heat the oven to 350°F/180°C/gas mark 4.

Roll out the pastry on a floured board. Grease and flour an 11-inch/25 cm pie dish and line it with the pastry. Pierce the base with a fork and sprinkle over about a tablespoon of the fresh breadcrumbs.

Grate the Italic cheese. Beat the eggs and milk in a bowl, season with salt and pepper and add the onions and cheese. Pour the mixture on to the pastry and bake in the lower part of the oven for 35-40 minutes. Serve hot.

Lettuce cigars

Savoury Canapés

Tartine Dolcipiccanti

To serve 4

2 oz/50 g butter, cut into small pieces

4 oz/100 g soft Gorgonzola cheese

1 teaspoon lemon juice

1 tablespoon chopped parsley

4 slices white bread

1 red pimiento

1 tender lettuce leaf, cut into strips

Preparation time: about 30 minutes

Beat the butter with a pinch of salt and pepper until creamy. Add the sieved and mashed Gorgonzola cheese and a teaspoon of lemon juice. Stir vigorously for a few minutes and then blend in the chopped parsley. Check and adjust the seasoning according to taste.

Spread the mixture on the slices of bread. Cut each slice in half diagonally to form 2 triangles and arrange on a plate. Cut the pimiento into 8 small strips and use to decorate the canapés. Garnish the centre of the plate with the strips of lettuce and serve immediately.

Polenta and Cheese Pudding

'Budino' di Polenta al Formaggio

To serve 6-8

¾ pint/450 ml milk

1½ stock cubes

12 oz/350 g quick-cooking polenta

2 oz/50 g butter

olive oil

4 oz/100 g grated Parmesan cheese

1 oz/25 g plain flour

2 egg yolks

4 oz/100 g Fontina cheese

celery leaves

Preparation and cooking time: about 40 minutes

Heat 2 pints/1.5 litres of water and ¼ pint/150 ml of milk. Add a little salt and crumble in a stock cube. As soon as the mixture begins to boil, sprinkle in the polenta, stirring first with a whisk and then a wooden spoon. Cook for about 20 minutes, then remove from

the heat. Mix in 1 oz/25 g of butter in small knobs and half the Parmesan cheese, stirring constantly. Put the polenta into a greased mould with fluted sides. Cover with a cloth and prepare the sauce.

Melt the remaining butter in a saucepan and incorporate the flour, mixing with a small whisk. Boil the remaining milk and combine it with the roux a little at a time. Stirring constantly, bring the sauce to the boil and flavour with half a stock cube. Remove from the heat and add the 2 egg yolks, the remaining Parmesan cheese and the Fontina cheese cut into small pieces. Mix well, then pour the boiling sauce over the polenta which has been turned out on to a deep dish. For garnish, place the chopped celery leaves in the centre of the polenta pudding and serve immediately. This substantial hot starter can also be served as a main course.

Polenta and cheese pudding

Cauliflower à la Grecque

Cavolfiore del Pireo

To serve 4-6

olive oil

juice of 2 large lemons

2 bay leaves

2 garlic cloves

3-4 black peppercorns

1½ lb/750 g cauliflower

Preparation and cooking time: about 1 hour plus chilling

Bring to the boil a large saucepan containing 1½ pints/800 ml cold water, add 6 tablespoons/100 ml of olive oil, the strained lemon juice, 2 bay leaves, 2 large halved garlic cloves, 3-4 black peppercorns and salt.

Meanwhile, wash the cauliflower and separate it into flowerets, without breaking them. Cook in the boiling liquid, with the pan covered and over a low heat, for about 12 minutes.

Remove the pan from the heat and, keeping it covered, let the flowerets cool. Only at this point remove the garlic and peppercorns (leave the bay leaves), then pour the preparation into a salad bowl. Cover it with cling film and keep it in the refrigerator for at least 1½ hours before serving. This starter, keeps well in the refrigerator for up to a week.

Mushrooms à la Grecque

Funghi di Coltura Ateniesi

To serve 6

¾-1 lb/400 g small fresh mushrooms

5 tablespoons strained lemon juice

olive oil

1 bay leaf

2 garlic cloves

large bunch of parsley

1 small stick celery

4-5 black peppercorns

1 red onion

Preparation and cooking time: about 50 minutes plus cooling

Trim the stems of the mushrooms and peel or wipe the caps. Rinse them well. Place on the heat a saucepan with 1 pint/500 ml of water, the lemon juice, 5 tablespoons of olive oil, bay leaf, 2 halved garlic cloves, 3-4 chopped parsley sprigs, the chopped celery, 4-5 peppercorns and a good pinch of salt; bring to the boil, then simmer for a couple of minutes, half-covered.

Meanwhile quarter the mushrooms, then plunge them into the liquid and simmer for about 15 minutes. Chop a small handful of parsley and cut 6 thin rings from the onion. When the mushrooms are ready pour them into a bowl with the hot cooking liquid, removing the garlic and bay leaf. Leave to cool at room temperature, then sprinkle with the chopped parsley, garnish with the onion rings and serve. These mushrooms, kept in the liquid and covered with cling film, will keep for 3-4 days in the refrigerator.

Cauliflower à la grecque

Rustic Tomatoes
Pomodori alla Rustica

To serve 4

2 tablespoons capers

1 onion

4 anchovy fillets

oregano

olive oil

12 oz/350 g tomatoes

Preparation time: about 40 minutes

Rinse the capers, peel the onion, cut it into as thin rings as possible, then keep them in cold water for about 30 minutes. Finely chop the anchovy fillets and place them in a bowl. Add a pinch of oregano, a grinding of pepper and a pinch of salt, then dilute with 5 tablespoons of olive oil, mixing vigorously with a fork. Set aside the dressing for a few minutes and prepare the tomatoes.

Wash and dry the tomatoes and cut them in rather thin slices. Drain the onion rings and the capers; dry them, separately, on kitchen paper. Place the tomato slices in a bowl, alternating them with the capers and onion rings, then pour over the prepared dressing and serve immediately, tossing gently.

Stuffed Baked Aubergines
Melanzane dello Skipper

To serve 4

2 large aubergines, together weighing about 1½ lb/750 g

1 small onion

2-3 fresh basil leaves

1 garlic clove

olive oil

8 oz/250 g firm ripe tomatoes

½ stock cube

4 heaped tablespoons breadcrumbs

1 tablespoon chopped parsley

2 tablespoons grated Pecorino cheese

Preparation and cooking time: about 1¾ hours.

Wash the aubergines and halve them lengthwise. Scoop out the flesh, leaving a border of about ½ inch/1 cm and being careful not to damage the skin. Cut the flesh into small pieces.

Chop the onion and basil and fry gently with a whole garlic clove in 4 tablespoons of olive oil. Stir in the pieces of aubergine and cook for a few minutes.

Chop the tomatoes finely, process them in a blender and add them to the pan. Season with the crumbled half stock cube and a little pepper. Cover the pan and cook on a moderate heat for about 20 minutes, stirring occasionally. Remove from the heat and leave to cool. Discard the garlic. Blend in 3 heaped tablespoons of fresh breadcrumbs, the chopped parsley and grated Pecorino cheese.

Pre-heat the oven to 375°F/190°C/gas mark 5. Stuff the aubergines with the prepared mixture and place them in an oiled ovenproof serving dish. Sprinkle with a tablespoon of breadcrumbs and a little olive oil. Cover the dish with foil and cook in the oven for about 1 hour. Remove the foil after about 45 minutes so that the aubergines can brown slightly on top. Serve either hot or cold.

Piquant Peppers

Peperoni Aromatici

To serve 6-8

8 small yellow sweet peppers, weighing about 2 lb/1 kg in all

2 oz/50 g capers

4 large anchovy fillets in oil

½ garlic clove

a handful of parsley

Tabasco sauce

Worcestershire sauce

1 tablespoon mustard

olive oil

Preparation and cooking time: about 50 minutes plus at least 2 hours' chilling

Gently grill the peppers and remove the scorched skin. Halve them, discarding the stalks and seeds, and flatten. Arrange in a single layer on a large plate.

Thoroughly drain the capers and chop coarsely, together with the anchovy fillets, half a garlic clove and a small handful of parsley. Sprinkle the mixture over the peppers.

Prepare the dressing: mix together a pinch of salt, 2-3 drops of Tabasco and a dash of Worcestershire sauce. Blend in a tablespoon of mustard, stirring with a fork. When the salt has completely dissolved, add 5 tablespoons of olive oil and blend to a smooth sauce.

Pour the prepared dressing over the peppers, cover with cling film and leave to stand in a cool place for at least 2 hours. This dish improves if left to stand and is best eaten a day after preparation.

Royal Aspic

Aspic Regale

To serve 12

1 small onion

1 clove

3 large carrots

1 small stalk celery

1 garlic clove

2-3 sprigs fresh parsley

¾-1 lb/350 g chicken on the bone

1 pint/500 ml prepared aspic gelatine
1 tablespoon gelatine, soaked,
added to an additional ½ pint/300 ml
prepared aspic gelatine

4 eggs

¾-1 lb/350 g potatoes

about 8 oz/250 g courgettes

6 oz/150 g cooked French beans

2 oz50 g tinned tuna in oil

2 tablespoons capers

2 anchovy fillets in oil

4 oz/100 g mayonnaise

1 teaspoon lemon juice

1 large red pimiento

8 oz/250 g ham, diced

Worcestershire sauce

1 tablespoon tomato ketchup

oil

Preparation and cooking time: about
1½ hours plus at least 4 hours'
refrigeration

Bring to the boil a saucepan containing
1½ pints/750 ml of water, the onion
(halved and pierced with a clove), 1 oz/
25 g diced carrot, the celery, a lightly
crushed garlic clove and the parsley,
salt it and add the chicken. Half-cover
the pan and simmer for about 50
minutes.

Meanwhile, prepare the aspic
according to instructions. Hard-boil the
eggs, cool under running water and
shell.

Peel and dice the potatoes and cook
them in salted boiling water for about
12 minutes. Drain and leave to dry on
kitchen paper, reserving the water. Cut
the courgettes into ⅛ inch/3 mm slices
and cook in the potato water for about
10 minutes. Drain and spread out on a
plate. Slice the remaining carrot and,
using the same water again, cook it for
about 15 minutes. Drain and dry.

Cut the French beans into ¾ inch/2
cm lengths. Bone and skin the chicken
and cut the meat into thin strips. Place
in a bowl and leave to cool.

Meanwhile, finely chop the tuna,
capers and anchovy fillets and place
them in a bowl. Stir in the mayonnaise
and lemon juice and use the mixture to
dress the chicken. Add 3-4
tablespoons of the cooled aspic.

Brush the inside of a 2½ pint/1.5 litre
hemispherical mould with the aspic
gelatine, coating it 3-4 times and
setting it in the refrigerator after each
coating.

Slice the hard-boiled eggs. Using a
pastry cutter, cut 6 tear-drop shapes
out of the pimiento. Line the mould with
some of the slices of egg, slices of
carrot and courgettes, cubes of potato
and tear-drops of pimiento. Fill the
mould with layers of the remaining
vegetables, the chicken mixture and
the rest of the slices of egg, pouring a
little aspic on top of each layer. By the
time all the ingredients and aspic have
been used up, the mould should be
almost full. Tap the mould gently and
then refrigerate for at least 4 hours or
until the aspic has set completely.

Meanwhile add the soaked gelatine
to the additional ½ pint/300 ml of aspic
while it is still hot and stir until the
gelatine has dissolved completely.
Liquidize. Pour the mixture into a
blender and add the diced ham, a
dash of Worcestershire sauce and the
tomato ketchup. Pour the mixture into a
9½-inch/24 cm round shallow
container which has been greased with
a little oil. Refrigerate for a couple of
hours to set. Turn out on to a plate.

Submerge the mould containing the
aspic in hot water for a few seconds,
dry it and then turn the aspic out on to
the ham. Garnish and serve.

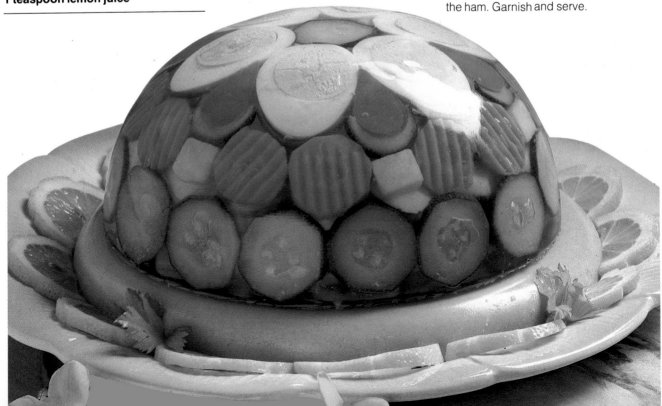

Stuffed Courgettes
Tronchetti di Zucchine

To serve 3

3 equal-sized courgettes

a little milk

1 slice very fresh white bread

4 oz/100 g minced lean beef

1 tablespoon pine-nuts

handful of parsley

2 garlic cloves

1 oz/25 g grated Parmesan cheese

1 egg yolk

ground nutmeg

olive oil

6 tablespoons/100 ml meat stock

2 tablespoons tomato juice

Preparation and cooking time: about 1¼ hours

Trim off the ends of the courgettes, wash and dry them, then cut each one into 3 chunks of equal size. Remove most of the pulp of each one (keep it for a soup or a cream of vegetables), making sure not to cut the outside green part.

Prepare the stuffing: soak the slice of white bread in a small amount of milk, then squeeze it and crumble it in a bowl. Add the minced beef, the pine-nuts, the finely chopped parsley mixed with half a garlic clove, the Parmesan cheese and the egg yolk. Mix everything together thoroughly, add salt and pepper and season with ground nutmeg.

Use this mixture to stuff the 9 pieces of courgette without overfilling them. Pre-heat the oven to 400°F/200°C/gas mark 6. Heat 4 tablespoons of oil in a frying pan and sauté a garlic clove. When the oil is hot, remove the garlic and throw it away, then place the chunks of courgette in the pan and fry them lightly on each side. Next arrange them in an ovenproof dish, just big enough to contain them all in one layer; moisten them with the stock mixed with the tomato juice and a tablespoon of oil. Cover the dish and put it in the oven for about 40 minutes, uncovering for the last 10 minutes. Transfer the courgettes to a warmed serving dish and serve.

Yellow Peppers with Aromatic Sauce
Peperoni Gialli con Trito d'Aromi

To serve 4

4 yellow peppers

1 garlic clove

anchovy paste

15 capers in vinegar

few sprigs parsley

1 sprig fresh watercress

Worcestershire sauce

olive oil

Preparation and cooking time: about 40 minutes plus at least 2 hours' resting

Wash and dry the peppers, then grill them to scorch the skins, turning them over. Then wrap them individually in a double sheet of kitchen paper and leave them to rest for about 10 minutes. Remove the paper and peel them completely, keeping them under running water. Dry and divide each pepper into 3 large strips, removing the seeds and the stem. Arrange the strips in a bowl, overlapping them slightly, and prepare the dressing.

Crush the garlic clove in a small bowl, add 1½ inches/3 cm of anchovy paste and the finely chopped capers, parsley sprigs and watercress leaves, a pinch of salt, a few drops of Worcestershire sauce and 5 tablespoons of olive oil. Pour the sauce over the pepper strips, cover the dish with cling film and leave it for at least 2 hours in a cool place. Serve the peppers sprinkled with chopped parsley in 2 or more small serving bowls.

Golden Aubergine Slices
Melanzane 'Indorate'

To serve 4-5

2 aubergines, each weighing about 12 oz/350 g

2 eggs

white pepper

2 oz/50 g grated Pecorino cheese

6 oz/150 g fresh breadcrumbs

flour

frying oil

Preparation and cooking time: about 40 minutes plus 1 hour's resting

Wash and dry the aubergines and cut them in slices about ½ inch/1 cm thick. Lay them on a large tray covered with kitchen paper and sprinkle them with salt to bring out their bitter juices. Leave them to rest in a cool place for about 1 hour, then wash and dry the slices.

Beat the eggs in a bowl with a pinch of salt and pepper. Mix the Pecorino cheese with the breadcrumbs. Roll each slice of aubergine in the flour, then dip it in the beaten eggs and then in the mixture of breadcrumbs and Pecorino cheese, making sure that each coating covers the slice completely. Heat plenty of vegetable oil in a frying pan; place the slices of aubergine in the pan a few at a time and brown. Remove them with a slotted spoon and, after draining, place them on a plate covered with a double sheet of kitchen paper to absorb the excess oil; continue to fry the others. Finally arrange the aubergine slices on a serving dish.

Stuffed courgettes (top left), *yellow peppers with aromatic sauce* (top right) and *golden aubergine slices*

Asparagus in Batter

Asparagi in Pastella, Fritti

To serve 6

3-3½ lb/1.5 kg fresh asparagus

4 oz/100 g flour

1 egg yolk

⅓ pint/200 ml fresh light cream

5 egg whites

oil for frying

Preparation and cooking time: about 1 hour

Peel and tail the asparagus and tie into a bundle with kitchen string. Stand the bundle upright in a saucepan containing a little salted boiling water and cook for about 15 minutes or until tender. Remove the string and spread the asparagus out to dry on kitchen paper.

Meanwhile prepare the batter: sift the flour into a bowl and add the egg yolk and a little salt. Gradually blend in the cream, stirring with a whisk. Beat the egg whites with a pinch of salt until stiff and then fold them into the batter mixture.

Cut the asparagus pieces in half, dip them in the batter and fry them in the hot oil until golden brown. Drain the asparagus on kitchen paper, arrange on a plate and sprinkle with salt. Serve immediately while still hot and crisp.

Asparagus au Gratin

Asparagi Gratinati

To serve 4

2½ lb/1.2 kg fresh asparagus

4 oz/100 g butter

1 oz/25 g flour

½ pint/300 ml meat stock

1 egg yolk

4 tablespoons whipping cream

3 oz/75 g grated Parmesan cheese

Preparation and cooking time: about 1 hour

Trim, peel and wash the asparagus and tie in a bundle with kitchen twine. Stand the bundle upright in a saucepan of enough salted boiling water to come halfway up the asparagus and cook for about 15 minutes. Drain, discard the twine and spread the asparagus out to dry and cool on absorbent kitchen paper. Preheat the oven to 400°F/200°C/gas mark 6.

Lightly butter a rectangular ovenproof dish which will hold the asparagus lengthwise. Melt 2 oz/50 g of the butter in a saucepan and stir in the flour to form a smooth roux. Gradually add the boiling stock and bring back to the boil, stirring constantly. Remove the pan from the heat and blend in the egg yolk and cream.

Arrange half the asparagus in the ovenproof dish and sprinkle on about 1 oz/25 g of the grated Parmesan cheese. Pour over half of the prepared sauce and sprinkle with about 1 oz/25 g of Parmesan cheese. Form a second layer in the same way using the remainder of the sauce and cheese.

Melt the remaining butter and pour it over the asparagus. Cook in the oven for about 15 minutes and serve immediately.

Asparagus with Vinaigrette

Asparagi Bianchi alla Castellana

To serve 4

3½ lb/1.5 kg fresh asparagus

anchovy paste

1 teaspoon mustard

1 tablespoon white wine vinegar

olive oil

Preparation and cooking time: about ¾ hour

Tail, scrape and wash the asparagus and tie in a bundle with kitchen twine. Stand the bundle upright in a saucepan of enough salted boiling water to come halfway up the asparagus and cook for about 12 minutes or until tender. Drain, discard the twine and spread the asparagus out to dry on kitchen paper.

Place in a bowl a generous pinch of salt and pepper, about 1 inch/2 cm of anchovy paste, a teaspoon of mustard and a tablespoon of wine vinegar. Stir with a fork until the salt has completely dissolved. Add 5 tablespoons of olive oil, stirring constantly.

Serve the asparagus, either hot or warm, with the prepared sauce.

Asparagus au gratin and *asparagus with vinaigrette*

Salad with Olives

Insalata Olivetta

To serve 4-5

1 small head Belgian endive

1 heart Batavian endive

1 head radicchio

2 tablespoons white wine vinegar

olive oil

1 oz/25 g capers

a little parsley

anchovy paste

2 oz/50 g small black olives in brine

a small piece of leek

Preparation time: about 20 minutes

Trim and wash the two sorts of endive and the radicchio. Drain and dry, keeping the different types separate. Break up the leaves and arrange in a salad bowl. Prepare the salad dressing: Mix the wine vinegar with a pinch of salt and pepper in a bowl, stirring until the salt is dissolved. Add, one tablespoon at a time, 6 tablespoons of olive oil, stirring vigorously to blend the ingredients. Chop the capers and a few leaves of parsley and add to the *vinaigrette* together with 1½-2 inches/4-5 cm of anchovy paste. Blend thoroughly.

To serve, place the olives in the centre of the salad bowl and arrange a few finely cut strips of leek on top of them. Pour over the dressing and toss.

Endive Flan

Sfogliata di Scarola

To serve 8

12 oz/350 g puff pastry

8 oz/250 g onions

1 garlic clove

2 oz/50 g butter

olive oil

4 oz/100 g smoked bacon

1½ lb/750 g Batavian endive, boiled and drained

1 stock cube

ground nutmeg

about 1 tablespoon breadcrumbs

6 oz/150 g grated Emmental cheese

3 eggs

3 tablespoons grated Parmesan cheese

flour

¼ pint/150 ml milk

Preparation and cooking time: about 1½ hours plus any thawing

Defrost the pastry if necessary. Thinly slice the onions, finely chop a garlic clove and fry gently in a knob of butter and 3 tablespoons of olive oil until transparent.

Cut the bacon into short, thin strips and coarsely chop the endive. Add first the bacon and then the endive to the onion and garlic. Cook for about 10 minutes, stirring frequently. Season with the crumbled stock cube and a little ground nutmeg and pepper.

Butter a 10 inch/25 cm round, fluted pie dish and line it with the pastry. Pierce the base with a fork and sprinkle over a heaped tablespoon of breadcrumbs. Pre-heat the oven to 400°F/200°C/gas mark 6.

Remove the endive mixture from the heat and blend in first the grated Emmental cheese and then 2 of the eggs, stirring vigorously. Pour the mixture into the pastry base and smooth the surface with the back of a spoon. Top with a tablespoon of grated Parmesan cheese.

Prepare a light béchamel sauce by melting ¾ oz/20 g of butter, stirring in ½ oz/15 g of flour and adding the milk. Season with salt and a little ground nutmeg. Blend in an egg yolk. Pour the sauce into the pie shell and sprinkle on 2 tablespoons of grated Parmesan cheese. Cook in the oven for about 40 minutes or until the pie is cooked and golden brown on top. Remove from the oven and leave to stand for about 10 minutes before serving.

Salad with olives

Cauliflower Quiche

Quiche di Cavolfiore

To serve 8

1 lb/500 g puff pastry

1 lb/500 g cauliflower

1 tablespoon breadcrumbs

4 oz/100 g smoked bacon, cut into thin slices

4 oz/100 g butter

olive oil

nutmeg

1 oz/25 g grated Emmental cheese

1 tablespoon chopped parsley

1½ oz/40 g sausage meat, skin removed

2 oz/50 g rindless Fontina cheese

1 oz/25 g flour

½ pint/300 ml milk

2 egg yolks

1 oz/25 g grated Parmesan cheese

Preparation and cooking time: about 1½ hours plus any thawing

Defrost the pastry if necessary. Boil the cauliflower in salted water in an uncovered pan for about 10 minutes. Remove from the water with a large slotted spoon, drain well and leave to dry on a dish covered with a double thickness of kitchen paper. Pre-heat the oven to 375°F/190°C/gas mark 5.

Roll out the pastry to a thickness of about ⅛ inch/3 mm and line a round, buttered pie dish, 10 inches/25 cm in diameter with it. Prick the bottom of the pastry with a fork, sprinkle with breadcrumbs and make an even layer of bacon slices.

Break up the cauliflower and sauté the flowerets gently in 1 oz/25 g of butter and 3 tablespoons of olive oil. Add a little salt and grated nutmeg. Arrange the cauliflower on top of the bacon. Sprinkle with the grated Emmental and the parsley. Crumble the sausage meat and sprinkle it about the cauliflower. Cut the Fontina into small pieces and scatter them among the cauliflower pieces. Prepare a béchamel sauce by melting a large knob of butter in a pan, stirring in the flour and then the milk. Season with salt and nutmeg. Remove from the heat and stir in the egg yolks and the Parmesan. Pour the sauce over the quiche.

Bake the pie for 40 minutes, in the lower part of the oven to ensure it is cooked all the way through. Remove the quiche carefully from the dish and place on a wooden serving board. Serve immediately, piping hot.

Gourmet Asparagus

Asparagi di Bassano alla Buongustaia

To serve 4

2½ lb/1.2 kg fresh asparagus

a few parsley leaves

4 oz/100 g butter

4 egg yolks

Preparation and cooking time: about 45 minutes

Wash and trim the asparagus and tie in a bundle with kitchen twine. Stand the bundle upright in a saucepan of salted boiling water (the water should come about halfway up the asparagus). Simmer over a moderate heat for about 15 minutes, or a little longer if the asparagus are very thick.

Drain thoroughly, discard the kitchen twine and spread the asparagus out to dry on kitchen paper. Arrange in warmed asparagus dishes and garnish with a few leaves of parsley.

Melt the butter, season with salt and pepper and pour into a well in the asparagus in each dish. Place 1 egg yolk in the centre of each well containing the melted butter. Serve immediately. Each diner should blend the butter and egg yolk to form a delicate sauce and use it as a dip.

Asparagus Quiche
Torta Salata di Asparagi

To serve 8

8 oz/250 g puff pastry

2¼ lb/1 kg fresh asparagus

4 oz/100 g raw ham, thinly sliced

4 oz/100 g Emmental cheese

2 oz/50 g butter

3 eggs

6 tablespoons/100 ml single cream

1 oz/25 g grated Parmesan cheese

grated nutmeg

a few sprigs fresh parsley for garnish

Preparation and cooking time: about 1½ hours plus any thawing time

Trim the asparagus and tie in a bundle with kitchen string. Stand the bundle upright in a saucepan of enough salted boiling water to come halfway up the bundle and cook for about 15 minutes or until tender. Remove the string and spread the asparagus out to dry on paper towels.

Roll out the pastry and use it to line a greased 9½ inch/24 cm flan dish. Line the bottom with the slices of raw ham and cover with the thinly sliced Emmental cheese. Chop the asparagus and fry it gently in the butter, then arrange it on the cheese.

Pre-heat the oven to 375°F/190°C/ gas mark 5. Beat the eggs with the cream, the grated Parmesan cheese, a pinch of salt and pepper and a little grated nutmeg. Pour this mixture into the pie shell. Cook in the lower part of the oven for about 40 minutes. Place the quiche on a large plate, surround it with sprigs of parsley and serve.

Artichoke and Swiss Cheese Pie
Sfogliata Vallese

To serve 6

8 oz/250 g puff pastry

a little butter

1 tablespoon breadcrumbs

6 oz/175 g rindless Appenzell cheese, thinly sliced

1 lb/500 g frozen or tinned artichoke hearts

2 oz/50 g grated Sbrinz cheese

3 large eggs

2-3 sprigs parsley

Preparation and cooking time: about 1 hour plus thawing

Defrost the puff pastry if necessary, roll it out and line a 9-inch/22 cm round buttered pie dish with it. Prick the base of the pastry with a fork, then sprinkle over a tablespoon of breadcrumbs and cover with the thin slices of Appenzell cheese. Pre-heat the oven to 375°F/ 190°C/gas mark 5.

Following the instructions on the packet, cook the artichoke hearts in boiling salted water, then drain and leave them to dry for a few minutes on a plate covered with a tea-towel. Liquidize the artichokes. Put the pulp in a bowl. Add the grated Sbrinz, the eggs, chopped parsley, a little salt and a grinding of pepper. Mix thoroughly, then pour the mixture into the pie dish over the cheese.

Bake for 35 minutes in the lower part of the oven until the pastry is cooked through. Remove the pie from the oven, leave it to rest for a few minutes and then serve.

Swiss Chard Pie

Spogliata di Coste e Uova

To serve 8-10

1 lb/500 g puff pastry

8 oz/250 g Swiss chard, green part only

½ small onion

2 oz/50 g butter

½ stock cube

grated nutmeg

6 oz/150 g ricotta cheese

4 oz/100 g minced ham

4 eggs plus 4 egg yolks

1 oz/25 g grated Parmesan cheese

1 oz/25 g flour

⅓ pint/200 ml milk

2 tablespoons breadcrumbs

Preparation and cooking time: about 1 hour 40 minutes plus any thawing time

Defrost the pastry, if necessary. Bring to the boil a little salted water in a large saucepan. Wash and drain the chard, plunge it into the boiling water and cook, covered, for 10 minutes. Drain and cool it under running water. Squeeze out excess moisture and chop finely.

Chop the onion and fry it gently in 1 oz/25 g of the butter without browning it. Add the chard and cook gently together, stirring occasionally with a wooden spoon. Season with the crumbled half stock cube and a pinch of ground nutmeg. Remove from the heat and allow to cool.

Preheat the oven to 375°F/190°C/ gas mark 5. Sieve the Ricotta into a large bowl and add the ham, the cooked chard, 3 whole eggs and the grated Parmesan. Stir briskly until all the ingredients are thoroughly combined and leave it to stand. Prepare a Béchamel sauce with the remaining butter, the flour and the milk; season with salt and nutmeg and add it to the mixture in the bowl, stirring well.

Butter a 10-inch/25 cm pie dish with fluted sides and line it with just over half the pastry rolled out very thinly. Trim the edges and sprinkle the breadcrumbs over the bottom. Fill it with the chard mixture, level it off and make 5 hollows in it with the back of a teaspoon. Fill each hollow with a raw egg yolk. Reserve the white of 1 egg. Roll out the rest of the pastry to make a lid and seal it well. Brush the top with the lightly beaten egg white and pierce the centre with a fork. Cook the pie in the oven for about 40 minutes, on a low shelf so that the pastry base gets cooked through. Serve immediately from the cooking dish.

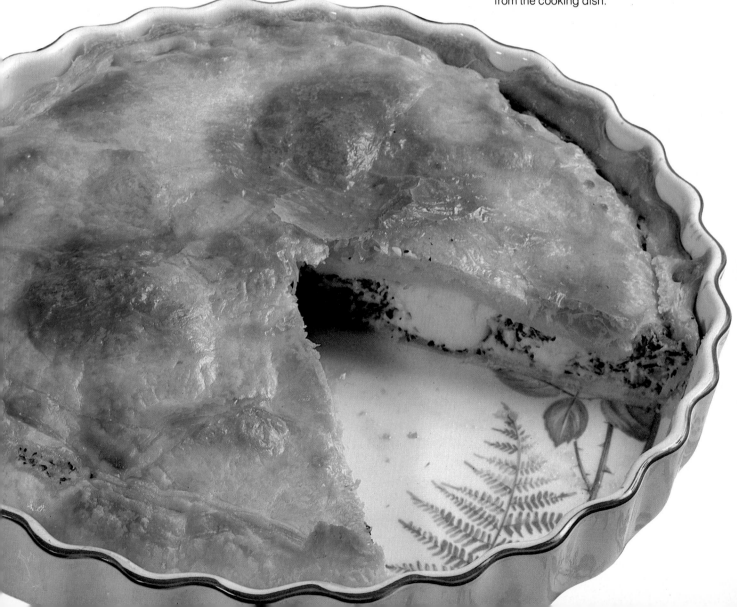

ANTIPASTI WITH

A delicious plate of wafer-thin slices of Parma ham and melon
is a classic *antipasto* dish, but a range of appetizers made
from Italian salami, hams, cured meats and seafoods — all
varying according to regional specialities — can find
themselves on the *antipasti* menu. Attractive to look at as well
as good to eat, they are often accompanied by olives,
hard-boiled eggs or anchovies.

SEAFOOD & MEAT

Lobster and Avocado
Aragosto e Avocado

To serve 4

4 oz/100 g boiled lobster meat

2 perfectly ripe avocados

Worcestershire sauce

2 teaspoons mustard

juice of ½ lemon

olive oil

4 crisp lettuce leaves

Preparation time: about 40 minutes

Dice the lobster into ½ inch/1 cm cubes and put them in a bowl. Cut the avocados in half lengthwise and remove the stones. Peel and slice them lengthwise and then cut into irregular-shaped pieces a little larger than the lobster cubes. Mix the two together carefully.

Prepare the dressing immediately: put a pinch of salt in a bowl and add a dash of Worcestershire sauce, the mustard and the strained lemon juice. Mix with a fork until the salt has completely dissolved. Then mix in 4 tablespoons of olive oil and continue stirring vigorously for a few minutes until the dressing emulsifies. Pour it over the lobster and avocado mixture, mix very carefully and leave for a few minutes. Place a lettuce leaf in each of 4 glass goblets and put some of the mixture in each goblet.

Lobster and Melon
Aragosto sul Melone

To serve 4

1 medium-sized sweet winter melon

8 oz/250 g boiled lobster meat

small glass port

3 oz/75 g mayonnaise

tomato ketchup

Preparation time: about 40 minutes

Cut the melon in half and remove the seeds and fibres. Scoop out the flesh in little balls and place these in a bowl. Cut the lobster into 12 medallions (not too thick) and dice the rest. Mix the diced lobster with the melon balls, pour in the port and mix carefully. Cover the bowl with cling film and refrigerate for about 10 minutes.

Arrange the melon and lobster mixture in 4 chilled goblets and place 3 medallions of lobster on top of each. Pipe a swirl of mayonnaise in the centre of each one. Serve accompanied by ketchup.

Lobster Tarts
Tartellette all'Aragosta

To serve 6

6 oz/150 g flour

¼ teaspoon yeast

2 oz/50 g butter

1 egg yolk

4 oz/100 g celeriac, peeled

4 oz/100 g fairly thick mayonnaise

1 teaspoon mustard

Worcestershire sauce

12 small medallions boiled lobster, weighing about 4 oz/100 g in all

Preparation and cooking time: about 1 hour

Pre-heat the oven to 375°F/190°C/gas mark 5. Sieve the flour on to a pastry-board and add a pinch of salt and the yeast. Mix, and make a well in the centre. Soften the butter and cut it into pieces. Put these, the egg yolk and 2 tablespoons of cold water into the well and mix quickly to a smooth dough.

Lightly flour a pastry-board and roll out the dough to a thickness of ⅛ inch/3 mm. Using a serrated 5-inch/13 cm round pastry cutter, cut out 6 rounds. Put these into buttered cup-shaped

moulds and prick the bases with a fork. Leave to rest and rise for 15 minutes. Bake for about 15 minutes until the pastry cases are golden brown. Remove from the oven and leave to cool in the moulds.

Meanwhile, shred the celeriac and mix immediately with half the mayonnaise, 1 teaspoon of mustard and a dash of Worcestershire sauce. When the pastry cases are cold, remove them from the moulds and place a little of the celeriac mixture in the bottom of each one. Lay two medallions of lobster on top, then pipe swirls of mayonnaise and garnish with a few lettuce leaves.

Savoy Cabbage with Smoked Salmon
Antipasto Pazzerello

To serve 4

2 leaves tender savoy cabbage

4 oz/100 g smoked salmon

3 oz/75 g Fiorello cheese

juice of ½ lemon

1 tablespoon tomato ketchup

1 tablespoon mustard

Worcestershire sauce

a little stock (or use stock cube)

Preparation time: about 30 minutes

Cut the salmon and cabbage into long strips. Prepare the dressing: Pour the Fiorello cheese into a bowl and whisk until slightly stiff. Add the lemon juice, the tomato ketchup and the mustard. Blend carefully and season with a pinch of salt and pepper and a generous splash of Worcestershire sauce. Stir in 2 tablespoons of stock and blend until smooth and creamy.

Arrange the strips of salmon and cabbage on a serving dish and dress with the sauce at the table. This is an unusual combination of ingredients, but the result is delicious and the dressing enhances the flavour of both the cabbage and the salmon.

Lobster and avocado (top left), *lobster and melon* (right) and *lobster tarts*

Chef's Roulades
Involtini dello Chef

To make 20 roulades

a handful of fresh parsley

8 oz/250 g very fresh Robiola cheese

Worcestershire sauce

20 very thin slices fillet of beef, weighing about 8 oz/250 g in all

olive oil

fresh rosemary

Preparation and cooking time: about 30 minutes

Pre-heat the oven to 475°F/250°C/gas mark 9. Finely chop the parsley and put in a bowl with the Robiola cheese, a little salt, a little freshly ground black pepper and a dash of Worcestershire sauce. Mix carefully to form a smooth paste. Lay out the slices of beef on a large tray and put a little of the cheese mixture in the centre of each one. Fold the meat over to make a little parcel so that the stuffing is sealed in. Sprinkle with salt and pepper.

Brush an ovenproof dish with olive oil and arrange the roulades on it, then pour a little olive oil over them. Place a few rosemary leaves on each one and put in the oven (or under the grill) for no longer than 1 minute to cook the meat without melting the cheese. Serve immediately.

Tasty Toast Appetizer
Fette Biscottate 'Golose'

To serve 4

6 oz/150 g tinned tuna in oil

¾ oz/20 g capers in vinegar

4 anchovy fillets in oil

3 oz/75 g thick mayonnaise

8 toasted bread slices

1 oz/25 g pimiento

a little fresh parsley

Preparation time: about 15 minutes

Drain the tuna fish, capers and anchovies. Roughly chop the capers and anchovies, mash the tuna and place everything in a bowl. Add the mayonnaise and stir well until all the ingredients are blended. Spread the mixture thickly over the toasted slices.

Drain, then chop the pimiento very finely, reducing it almost to a pulp, and place 1 teaspoon on each slice. Garnish with fresh parsley, arrange the slices on a tray and serve at once.

Little Savoury Pasties
"Crescentine" di Grasso

To serve 6-8

1 sprig fresh rosemary

2 oz/50 g mortadella sausage, finely chopped

2 oz/50 g salami, finely chopped

1 egg

1 oz/25 g grated Parmesan cheese

ground nutmeg

8 oz/250 g flour

½ teaspoon baking powder

butter

6 tablespoons/100 ml cold stock (or use stock cube)

1 egg white, lightly beaten

frying oil

Preparation and cooking time: about 1 hour

Chop the rosemary leaves finely and bind with the mortadella, salami, egg and grated Parmesan cheese. Season with a pinch of ground nutmeg and a little pepper.

Sift the flour, baking powder and a pinch of salt on to a board and make a well in the centre. Cut 1 oz/25 g of butter into small pieces and rub into the flour. Add the stock a little at a time and mix to form a soft pastry dough.

Roll the pastry out and cut it into 2½-3 inch/6-7 cm rectangles with a serrated pastry cutter. Brush the edges of the rectangles with the beaten egg white. Place a little of the prepared stuffing mixture in the centre of half of the rectangles and then cover with the remaining pieces of pastry. Press the edges together and seal carefully.

Heat plenty of oil in a large frying pan and fry the pasties until golden brown on both sides. Drain and dry on kitchen paper. Place in a large dish and serve immediately.

Little savoury pasties

Salmon and Crab Rolls

Involtini di Salmone al Granchio

To serve 6

6 oz/175 g smoked salmon

6 oz/175 g crab meat

Worcestershire sauce

3 oz/80 g mayonnaise

1 tablespoon mustard

Tabasco sauce

a little gelatin dissolved in 6 tablespoons/100 ml warm water

celery leaves

1 pimiento

2 slices lemon

Preparation time: about 40 minutes

Divide the smoked salmon into 18 slices and spread them out on a large sheet of foil. Drain and squeeze the crab well, then put it in a bowl and remove any filaments or bits of cartilage. Flavour with a generous dash of Worcestershire sauce, the mayonnaise, mustard and 2 or 3 drops of Tabasco. Stir thoroughly, then place some of the mixture on one edge of each slice of salmon and roll the salmon up tightly.

Arrange the rolls neatly on a serving dish and brush them all two or three times with the gelatin, refrigerating between applications to help the gelatin to set. Garnish the dish with the celery leaves, pimiento and lemon slices. Cover the dish with cling film and keep it in the refrigerator until it is time to serve it.

Stuffed Grapefruit

Pompelmi Ripieni

To serve 6

3 medium-sized grapefruit

2 kiwi fruit

2 oz/50 g Emmental cheese

2 thick slices ham

3 oz/80 g mayonnaise

Worcestershire sauce

2 tablespoons mustard

Preparation time: about 40 minutes

Using a short, sharp knife, cut the grapefruit into halves. Separate them, scoop out the pulp and put it in a bowl, taking care not to include any pith. Peel the kiwi fruit, halve them lengthwise and slice thinly. Cut the Emmental cheese into matchsticks and the ham into short strips. Pour off the juice that has run out of the grapefruit and mix the flesh with the kiwi fruit, cheese and ham. Put the mayonnaise in a bowl, flavour it with a dash of Worcestershire sauce and the mustard and stir into the prepared mixture. Fill the grapefruit halves with the mixture, serve at once.

Salmon Canapés

Tartine Salmonate

To make 16 canapés

3 oz/75 g smoked salmon

2 oz/50 g fresh Mascarpone cheese

1 tablespoon Framboise liqueur

2 tablespoons single cream

1 tablespoon tomato ketchup

Worcestershire sauce

8 slices white bread

a few olives in brine

a few chicory leaves

Preparation time: about 20 minutes

Process the salmon in a liquidizer and place in a bowl. Mix in the Mascarpone cheese and the Framboise liqueur. Stir in the cream and tomato ketchup. Season with a few drops of Worcestershire sauce.

Spread a heaped tablespoon of the mixture on each slice of bread, spreading it right to the edges. Cut the slices of bread in half diagonally to form triangles.

Slice a few olives lengthwise and use to garnish the canapés, together with a few leaves of chicory if desired. The canapés may be served as an hors-d'oeuvre or as an accompaniment to apéritifs.

Egg with Tuna Fish and Peas

Uova al Tonno e Piselli

To serve 4

6 oz/150 g frozen young peas

1 small onion

olive oil

about 6 oz/175 g tinned tuna fish

4 eggs

Preparation and cooking time: about 25 minutes

Boil the peas, still frozen, in salted water for 5 minutes, then drain them. Peel and finely slice the onion, then fry in 2 tablespoons of olive oil on a low heat until transparent. Add the peas and leave. Drain the tuna fish of oil and mash it coarsely. Add it to the peas and leave over the heat for 7-8 minutes.

Meanwhile heat 2 tablespoons of olive oil in a large frying pan and break in the eggs, which should be at room temperature, taking care not to break the yolks. Add a little salt and pepper, and turn the heat down low. Cook until the whites are opaque. Remove the eggs one at a time with a flexible spatula and drain off any excess oil.

Place each egg on a warm plate and surround with the tuna fish and pea mixture. Serve at once.

Stuffed grapefruit (top) and *salmon and crab rolls*

Little Chicken Pasties
Piccoli Calzoni Ripieni di Pollo

To make 24 pasties

2 slices white bread soaked in milk

4 oz/100 g chicken breast, trimmed

fresh chives

a little fresh parsley

4-5 sprigs fresh chervil

1 oz/25 g grated Parmesan cheese

1 egg

nutmeg

1 lb/500 g bread dough

a little flour

frying oil

Preparation and cooking time: about 45 minutes

Squeeze out the milk from the bread and mince it finely with the chicken. Finely chop 6-8 chives together with 2-3 large sprigs of parsley and 4-5 sprigs of chervil. Add the herbs to the chicken mixture. Add the Parmesan, the egg, salt, pepper and a little grated nutmeg. Mix thoroughly.

Roll out the bread dough, a little at a time, on a lightly floured pastry-board to about 1 inch/2 cm thickness. Using a pastry cutter cut out rounds 5 inches/12 cm in diameter. Place a little of the chicken mixture on one side of each round, then fold it in half and seal by pinching the two edges together. As the pasties are ready, line them up on a tray covered with a lightly floured cloth.

Heat a deep frying pan with plenty of oil. When the oil is hot, but not smoking, put in the pasties, a few at a time, and cook until they are golden brown. Drain them as you lift them from the oil and lay them on a plate covered with kitchen paper.

Smoked salmon with tuna fish *(top);* ***sturgeon cornets*** *(centre);* ***little chicken pasties*** *(bottom)*

Tuna mousse

into a bowl and add 2 drops of vinegar and a dash of Worcestershire sauce. Incorporate 1 tablespoon of mayonnaise. Spread on one side only of the toast fingers. Press a smoked salmon roulade firmly on to each piece of toast. Arrange on a dish and garnish.

Tuna Mousse
Anello di Tonno

To serve 6

½ sachet aspic jelly

about 12 oz/350 g tinned tuna in oil

butter

1 tablespoon flour

¼ pint/150 ml milk

juice of ½ lemon

oil

8 oz/250 g mayonnaise

3 tablespoons whipping cream

1 tablespoon tomato ketchup

Worcestershire sauce

Preparation and cooking time: about 30 minutes plus chilling
Prepare the aspic according to instructions with ¼ pint/150 ml of water. Leave to cool. Drain the tuna and mash it finely in a bowl.

Melt 1 oz/25 g butter in a small saucepan and blend in a tablespoon of flour. Gradually add the milk and bring almost to the boil, stirring constantly. The sauce should be thick and smooth. Remove from the heat, season with a little salt and blend with the mashed tuna. Add the lemon juice and stir well.

Add the prepared aspic and stir vigorously. Pour the mixture into a 2½ pint/1.5 litre ring mould which has been lightly oiled. Place in the freezer for 40 minutes.

Prepare the sauce: pour the mayonnaise into a bowl and blend in the cream, tomato ketchup and a few drops of Worcestershire sauce. Test and adjust the seasoning to taste.

Turn the tuna mousse out on to a round plate and coat it with the prepared sauce. Garnish as desired and serve.

Sturgeon Cornets
'Cornetti' di Storione

To serve 4

1 egg

a little fresh parsley

1 anchovy fillet in oil

2 green olives, stoned

1 tablespoon mayonnaise

8 very thin slices smoked sturgeon

toasted wholemeal bread

Preparation and cooking time: about 30 minutes
Hard-boil the egg, then cool under cold running water. Shell and finely chop it, then put in a bowl. Finely chop a little parsley together with the drained anchovy fillet and the olives and add to the egg. Add the mayonnaise and mix to a smooth paste. Taste and adjust the seasoning, then spread the mixture on one side of each fish slice. Roll the slice into a funnel shape, sealing in the filling. When all the 'cornets' are ready, fan them out on a round serving dish and garnish to taste. Serve with slices of warm toasted wholemeal bread.

Smoked Salmon with Tuna Fish
Salmone Tonnata

To serve 6

10 capers

10 gherkins

4 oz/100 g tinned tuna fish in oil

2 tbsp mayonnaise

¼ tsp mustard

6 large slices smoked salmon

2 slices wholemeal bread

anchovy paste

a little white wine vinegar

Worcestershire sauce

lettuce leaves for garnish

Preparation and cooking time: about 40 minutes
Drain the capers and gherkins thoroughly and chop them finely, together with the well-drained tuna fish. Add 1 tablespoon of mayonnaise and the mustard and mix thoroughly. Spread this on the salmon slices, taking care not to go over the edges. Using the blade of a knife, roll up the salmon into 6 roulades and put them in the least cold part of the refrigerator for a few minutes.

Meanwhile, toast the bread and cut each slice into 3 fingers. Squeeze about 1¼ inches/3 cms anchovy paste

Tuna Delight
Delizia di Tonno

To serve 6

1 gelantine sachet (to make 1 pint/600 ml)

1 tablespoon lemon juice

1 egg

12 oz/350 g tinned tuna

1½ tablespoons capers

4 anchovy fillets in oil

Worcestershire sauce

a little oil

a few leaves chicory

1 red pepper, cut into strips

Preparation and cooking time: about 1 hour
Dissolve the gelatine in ¾ pint/450 ml of hot water and add a tablespoon of lemon juice. Hard-boil the egg, shell and chop it and blend with the well-drained tuna, the drained capers, the anchovy fillets, a dash of Worcestershire sauce and the gelatine. Blend gently for a couple of minutes.

Oil a 2-pint/1-litre fluted mould and pour in the tuna mixture. Place the mould in the refrigerator and allow the mixture to set. Turn out, slice it and arrange on a large plate. Garnish with strips of red pepper and sprigs of chicory.

Melon and Prawns
Melone e Gamberetti

To serve 6

6 tablespoons/100 ml dry white wine

1 small bay leaf

2-3 whole black peppercorns

2-3 sprigs fresh parsley

1 small onion, halved

12 oz/350 g prawns

1 medium-sized melon

2 tender lettuce leaves

5 oz/125 g thick mayonnaise

2 tablespoons mustard

2 tablespoons tomato ketchup

1 tablespoon whipping cream

Worcestershire sauce

1 teaspoon brandy

Preparation and cooking time: about 1 hour
Bring to the boil a saucepan containing 1 pint/500 ml of water, a little salt, the white wine, bay leaf, peppercorns, parsley and onion and simmer for at least 5 minutes. Add the prawns, cook for about 4 minutes and then remove them from the pan with a slotted spoon, discarding the other ingredients. When the prawns have cooled, peel them and place them in a bowl.

Cut the melon in half using a sharp, pointed knife. Discard the seeds. Scoop out the flesh, cut into ½-inch/1 cm cubes and place in a bowl. Put a lettuce leaf in the bottom of each empty melon rind.

Prepare the dressing: blend the mayonnaise with the mustard, tomato ketchup, cream, a dash of Worcestershire sauce and the brandy. Test and adjust the seasoning according to taste.

Mix the prawns and melon cubes and dress with the prepared sauce. Divide the mixture between the 2 halves of melon and serve immediately.

Tuna delight

Melon with prawns (right)

Prawn Pie
Sfogliata di Gamberetti

8 oz/250 g puff pastry

butter

1 tablespoon breadcrumbs

6 slices very fresh white bread

6 tablespoons/100 ml milk

12 oz/350 g prawns, unpeeled

olive oil

1 garlic clove

2-3 tablespoons dry white wine

1 small onion

a handful of parsley

2 eggs

Preparation and cooking time: about 1¼ hours plus any thawing time
Preheat the oven to 375°F/190°C/gas mark 5. Defrost the pastry if necessary. Line a buttered 10 x 4 inch/25 × 10 cm pie dish with the pastry and prick with a fork. Sprinkle with the breadcrumbs. Arrange the slices of bread on a plate and soak for at least 15 minutes in the milk. Peel the prawns and sauté them in a frying pan with 1 tablespoon of olive oil and ½ garlic clove. Season with salt and pepper. Pour in 2 or 3 tablespoons of wine and wait until it has evaporated before removing the prawns from the heat and leaving to cool.

Finely chop the onion with a small handful of parsley and fry in 3 tablespoons of olive oil and a little salt. Put these ingredients in a bowl. Break in the eggs and beat well. Add the bread soaked in milk and break up into small pieces. Beat well until smooth. Finally, add the prawns and season with a little salt and pepper.

Pour the mixture into the pie dish and level it. Tap the dish lightly to remove any air bubbles. Bake in the lower part of the oven for about 35 minutes. Remove the pie from the oven and turn out on to a serving dish or wooden board and serve at once.

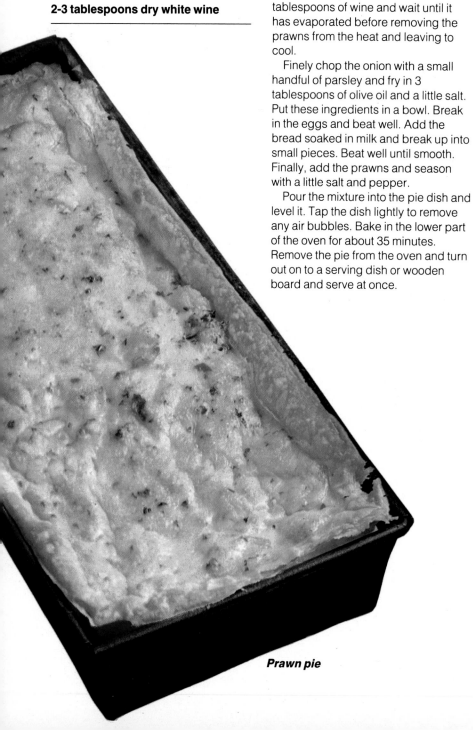

Prawn pie

Christmas Pâté
'Delizia' delle Feste

To serve 6-8

4 oz/100 g chicken livers

8 oz/200 g pork loin

1 medium leek, white part only

4 oz/100 g butter

olive oil

4 tablespoons dry Marsala wine

½ stock cube

4 oz/100 g raw ham

1 teaspoon white truffle paste

1 tablespoon pine-nuts

1 small black truffle

a little gelatine dissolved in water

toast

Preparation and cooking time: about 1¼ hours
Remove any traces of gall from the chicken livers, then carefully wash and drain them. Cut the pork loin into small slices. Finely slice the leek and fry in 2 oz/50 g of the butter and 1 tablespoon of olive oil, taking care not to let it brown. Then add the chicken livers and the pork, turn up the heat and allow to brown a little. Pour in the Marsala and crumble in the stock cube, stirring continuously with a wooden spoon.

When the Marsala has been completely absorbed, remove the frying pan from the heat and pour the contents into a blender. Add the chopped raw ham with the white truffle paste and the remaining butter cut into slivers. Blend on minimum speed for a minute and then on maximum for a couple of minutes. Sieve through a fine mesh into a bowl and leave to cool, stirring from time to time.

Mix again, vigorously, with a wooden spoon to make the pâté light and fluffy. Heap into 2 earthenware pâté dishes and garnish one with the pine-nuts and the other with slices of black truffle. Finally, brush the surface with the gelatine. As soon as it sets, cover the dishes with cling film and refrigerate. Serve with toast.

Artichoke and Prawn Salad

Insalata di Carciofi e Gamberetti

To serve 4

4 small artichokes

2 juicy lemons

olive oil

1 tablespoon white wine vinegar

8 oz/250 g fresh prawns, unpeeled

Preparation and cooking time: about 1 hour

Trim the artichokes, removing the tough outer leaves, the tips and the stalks. (You can save the latter for a soup or risotto.) Cut the artichokes in half, remove the chokes and immerse them in cold water to which a little lemon juice has been added. Heat a saucepan containing 2 pints/1 litre of water and add salt as soon as it begins to boil. Put in 1 teaspoon of lemon juice and 1 tablespoon of olive oil. Cut the artichoke halves into fairly thin slices and put them into the boiling water for 3 minutes. Remove with a slotted spoon. Drain and leave them to dry on a sloping dish.

Boil the prawns for 3 minutes in salted boiling water with a tablespoon of vinegar added, then drain, peel and leave them to cool. Mix the prawns with the artichokes in a bowl and make a dressing with a pinch of salt, a little freshly ground pepper, 1 tablespoon of strained lemon juice and 4 tablespoons of olive oil. Mix and serve garnished with scalloped half-slices of lemon.

Artichoke and prawn salad (top)
Christmas pâté (left)

Marine-style Clams
Cappe Chione alla Marinara

To serve 6

24 fresh clams

1 bay leaf

8 white peppercorns

2-3 sprigs fresh parsley

1 small onion

1 garlic clove

3 tbsp olive oil

4 tbsp white wine

2 egg yolks

6 tbsp/100 ml whipping cream

Preparation and cooking time: about 40 minutes plus at least 2 hours' soaking

Soak the clams in plenty of lightly salted cold water for at least two hours, frequently turning them and changing the water at least twice. Finally wash them well, one by one, under running water, placing them in a saucepan as they are done.

Cover them with cold water and add the bay leaf, peppercorns and almost all the parsley. Bring gradually to the boil, keeping the lid on but stirring from time to time. Take them off the heat, lift them out, rinse again in the cooking water if there is any trace of sand and keep them covered in a large deep serving dish.

Chop the onion and garlic finely and fry them gently in the oil, taking care not to brown them. Pour in the white wine and half a glass of the clams' cooking water strained through a cloth. Simmer for 5 or 6 minutes, then thicken with the egg yolks beaten together with the cream. Taste the sauce (which will be fairly runny), adjust the seasoning, pour it over the clams, sprinkle with chopped parsley and serve at once.

It is essential that all the sand is eliminated from the clams and that they should not be overcooked – being somewhat leathery by nature, they would then become inedible.

Mussels and King Prawns
Datteri e Mazzancolle 'Sapore di Mare'

To serve 4

1¼ lb/600 g mussels

12 king prawns

1 shallot

1 small carrot

1 stalk celery

1 garlic clove

2 whole black peppercorns

¼ bay leaf

3-4 tablespoons dry white wine

olive oil

1 tablespoon brandy

½ teaspoon cornflour

a few chives

Preparation and cooking time: about 1¼ hours

Thoroughly scrub the mussels and soak them in cold salted water for at least 30 minutes. Peel the prawns and place in a small saucepan. Add the chopped shallot, the carrot and celery, a lightly crushed garlic clove, peppercorns and a quarter of a bay leaf. Pour on 1 pint/500 ml of water and the wine. Season with a little salt, half-cover the pan and simmer gently for about 15 minutes. Strain the liquid into a frying pan and leave the prawns to cool.

Thoroughly drain the mussels and place them in the frying pan with the strained liquid. Cover the pan and heat briskly to open the shells. Remove the mussels to a plate, cover and keep hot.

Strain the remaining liquid into a bowl. Wash and dry the frying pan and heat 3-4 tablespoons of olive oil in it. Fry the prawns gently for a few minutes and then pour on a tablespoon of brandy. When the brandy has evaporated, add the strained liquid. Stir in half a teaspoon of cornflour dissolved in 2 tablespoons of cold water. Simmer for a few minutes and then add the mussels. Stir and cook for 3-4 minutes. Sprinkle with the chopped chives and serve with hot toast.

Marine-style clams

Fried Prawns with Herbs

Gamberetti in 'Scapece'

To serve 4-6

frying oil

1-1¼ lb/600 g prawns, peeled and washed

flour

2 shallots

2 fresh sage leaves

1 sprig fresh chervil

olive oil

¼ pint/150 ml white wine vinegar

¼ pint/150 ml dry white wine

2-3 whole black peppercorns

1 bay leaf

parsley for garnish

Preparation and cooking time: about 1 hour plus 12 hours' chilling

Heat plenty of oil in a large frying pan. Coat the prawns in flour and fry them rapidly in the oil until crisp and golden. Drain on kitchen paper and sprinkle with salt.

Finely chop the shallots, 2 large sage leaves and a few small leaves of chervil and sauté in the olive oil. Pour on the vinegar and white wine and add the peppercorns, bay leaf and a little salt. Simmer on a moderate heat for about 10 minutes.

Meanwhile, arrange the prawns in a serving dish, strain the prepared sauce and pour it over them. Leave to cool at room temperature and then cover the dish and chill in the refrigerator for at least 12 hours before serving. Garnish with a few leaves of parsley and serve.

Fried prawns with herbs (top) *and* mussels and king prawns

Mussels with a Sea Tang

Cozze al Sapore di Mare

To serve 6

6½ lb/3 kg fresh mussels

4-6 shallots

½ celery heart

4 oz/100 g mushrooms

a handful of parsley

1 tablespoon chopped chives

butter

¼ pint/150 ml dry white wine

nutmeg

cornflour

a few drops lemon juice

Preparation and cooking time: about 1½ hours

Scrape the mussels with a small knife under running water, then leave them in a bowl of salted cold water for at least 30 minutes. Meanwhile, finely chop the shallots with the celery, mushrooms and a handful of parsley. Add the finely chopped chives and fry in butter, taking care not to let the ingredients brown. Then put the mussels into the pan, pour in the wine, season generously with freshly ground black pepper and a little grated nutmeg. Cover the pan and allow the mussels to open over a high heat, shaking the pan from time to time.

Remove from the heat as soon as the mussels have opened. Take the mussels from their shells and place on a serving dish. Strain the liquid from the pan through muslin, then heat it until it has reduced by half. Add the rest of the butter, softened, in small pieces. Dissolve half a teaspoon of cornflour in 2 or 3 tablespoons of cold water and a few drops of lemon juice and add this too. Simmer gently for a few seconds, then pour over the mussels and sprinkle generously with chopped parsley. Serve immediately, garnishing the dish to taste.

Savoury Anchovies

Acciughe 'in Savore'

To serve 4-6

1½ lb/750 g very fresh anchovies

flour

frying oil

2 large onions

2 large garlic cloves

1 sprig fresh rosemary

1 bay leaf

3-4 peppercorns

a piece of cinnamon stick

olive oil

¼ pint/150 ml white wine vinegar

¾ pint/450 ml dry white wine

1 stock cube

1 leek, green part only

Preparation and cooking time: about 1½ hours plus 36 hours' marinading

Remove the heads from the anchovies, slit and gut the fish. Wash them rapidly under running water and drain carefully. Flour them, a few at a time, and shake off any excess flour. Heat plenty of oil in a deep-frying pan and fry the anchovies until they are browned all over. Drain from the oil and lay on a plate covered with a double layer of kitchen paper to absorb the excess oil. Lightly sprinkle with salt.

Meanwhile, finely slice the onions. Make a small muslin bag and place inside the lightly crushed garlic, rosemary, bay leaf, peppercorns and cinnamon. Secure the bag firmly. Heat 3 tablespoons of olive oil in a frying pan and put in first the bag of herbs and then the onion. Fry gently, stirring with a wooden spoon. As soon as the onions begin to brown, pour in the vinegar and the wine. Mix and bring slowly to the boil, then turn down the heat and cover the pan. Leave to simmer for about 15 minutes. Add salt 5 minutes before removing the pan from the heat.

Crumble in the stock cube. Remove the bouquet garni and squeeze it out well. Place the anchovies and the

boiling marinade in a deep dish and leave to cool, first at room temperature and then in the least cold compartment of the refrigerator for at least 36 hours. Be sure to cover the dish. Before serving, slice the leek into thin rings and use for garnish.

Avocado Hors-d'oeuvre

Antipasto di Avocado

To serve 6

4 oz/100 g prawns

6 tablespoons/100 ml white wine

1 bay leaf

parsley

peppercorns

a little mayonnaise

Worcestershire sauce

mustard

3 avocados

1 large lemon

Belgian endive

Preparation and cooking time: about 40 minutes

Heat ¼ pint/150 ml of water and the white wine in a saucepan, add the bay leaf, 3 sprigs of parsley, 2 black peppercorns and salt. Simmer for a few seconds, then turn down the heat and pour the prawns into the shallow boiling liquid, cover and boil for a couple of minutes. Remove them with a slotted spoon, drain well and leave to cool. Then put them in a bowl with a little mayonnaise, a generous dash of Worcestershire sauce and 2 teaspoons of mustard.

Cut the avocados in two and remove the stones. Using a teaspoon, scrape out some of the flesh and add it to the prawns. Finally, stir in a few drops of lemon juice. Place the mixture in the hollowed-out avocados and arrange on a serving dish. Decorate with mayonnaise. Place ½ slice of lemon between each avocado with some chopped endive. In the centre, place half a lemon decorated with mayonnaise. Serve at once.

Ham and Endive Rolls

Involtini di Indivia

To serve 4

4 large heads Belgian endive, together weighing about 1¼ lb/600 g

2 oz/50 g butter

a little dry white wine

8 bacon slices, sliced lengthwise

2 oz/50 g Emmental cheese

Preparation and cooking time: about 1½ hours

Trim and wash the endive and cut them in half lengthwise. Cook in salted boiling water for about 10 minutes. Drain and leave to dry on kitchen paper.

Melt the butter in a large frying pan. Cut the endives in half again lengthwise and fry briskly in the butter until golden brown. Pour on a little white wine and remove the pan from the heat as soon as the wine has evaporated. Drain the endive and leave to cool.

Preheat the oven to 350°F/180°C/gas mark 4. Wrap each piece of endive in a bacon strip, leaving the tip free. Arrange the rolls tip to tail in a buttered ovenproof dish. Dot with strips of Emmental cheese and bake for about 20 minutes or until the bacon is lightly crisped. Serve.

Ham and endive rolls (top)

Asparagus with Anchovies

Asparagi Verdi all'Acciuga

To serve 4

2¼ lb/1 kg fresh asparagus

anchovy paste

Worcestershire sauce

2 tablespoons white wine vinegar

olive oil

10 anchovy fillets for garnish

5 green olives, stoned and halved, for garnish

1 lemon, sliced, for garnish

Preparation and cooking time: about 1 hour

Trim the asparagus and rub gently to remove the outer skin. Wash, tie in a bundle and stand upright in a saucepan of salted boiling water (the water should come about halfway up the asparagus). Cook for about 15 minutes or until tender.

Drain and untie the asparagus and cut into 3 inch/75 mm lengths. Spread out to dry on paper towels.

Prepare the sauce: place 3 inches/75 mm of anchovy paste in a bowl with a pinch of salt and a generous dash of Worcestershire sauce. Add the wine vinegar and stir with a fork until the salt has completely dissolved. Blend in 5 tablespoons of olive oil, stirring vigorously.

Arrange the hot asparagus in a warmed serving dish, dress with the prepared sauce and mix carefully. Garnish with the anchovy fillets wrapped round the halved olives and with half-slices of lemon. Serve immediately.

Stuffed Tomatoes au Gratin

Pomodori all'Uovo, Gratinati

To serve 6

3 very large tomatoes

3 eggs

6 oz/175 g tinned tuna in oil

3 oz/75 g fresh breadcrumbs

1oz/25 g grated Parmesan cheese

1 large sprig parsley, finely chopped

1 garlic clove, finely chopped

a little oil

Preparation and cooking time: about 1 hour 20 minutes

Cut the tomatoes in half using a sharp knife and discard the seeds. Sprinkle the insides with a little salt and place the tomatoes upside-down on paper.

Hard-boil the eggs, cool under running water and shell them. Crumble the egg yolks and mix them with the drained tuna, the breadcrumbs, the grated Parmesan cheese and the chopped parsley and garlic. Season with a pinch of salt and blend.

Pre-heat the oven to 375°F/190°C/ gas mark 5. Stuff the tomatoes with the prepared mixture and arrange them in a lightly oiled baking tray. Pour on a little oil, cover with foil and cook in the oven for 20 minutes. Remove the foil and cook for a further 15 minutes or until the stuffed tomatoes are golden brown on top.

Arrange on a warmed dish and serve immediately while still piping hot. This dish is excellent as an hors-d'oeuvre or as an accompanying vegetable for a main course.

Stuffed Cod

'Picaia' di Merluzzo

To serve 6-8

4 fresh cod fillets, weighing about 1¾ lb/800 g in all

3 large garlic cloves

large bunch fresh parsley

4 oz/100 g fine breadcrumbs

2 oz/50 g grated Parmesan cheese

2 eggs

olive oil

Preparation and cooking time: about 1¼ hours

Pre-heat the oven to 375°F/190°C/gas mark 5. Lightly beat the cod fillets and overlap them a little so as to form a rectangle with an even edge. Sprinkle with salt and pepper. Finely slice a large garlic clove and scatter over the cod. Wash and dry the parsley and chop it very finely together with 2 garlic cloves. Place in a bowl. Add the breadcrumbs and Parmesan cheese, a pinch of salt and a generous sprinkling of freshly ground pepper. Mix well and add the eggs and 2 tablespoons of olive oil. Work into a smooth mixture and spread this evenly over the fish.

Using the blade of a long knife, raise the slab of fish, from the shorter edge, and roll it up tightly enough to keep the stuffing inside. Wrap the roll in a double sheet of oiled foil, sealing the ends and then the upper edges. Tie up with kitchen string, as for a roast. Place the roll in a casserole that is just the right size and bake in the oven for about 45 minutes, carefully turning the roll from time to time. Serve either hot by itself or cold with mayonnaise.

Cold Fish Mousse

Sformato di Pesce, Freddo

To serve 8

1 oz/25 g gelatine

4 oz/100 g monkfish, cut into walnut-sized pieces

flour

butter

olive oil

1 large onion

2 garlic cloves

8 oz/250 g prawns, heads removed

6 tablespoons/100 ml dry white wine

1 pint/500 ml fish stock

Preparation and cooking time: about 40 minutes plus overnight refrigeration

Dissolve the gelatine in a little cold water. Lightly flour the monkfish pieces and cook them very gently in 1 oz/25 g of butter and 2 tablespoons of olive oil, without browning them. Add a little salt and leave on a plate to cool. Finely chop the onion with the garlic and sauté them in the frying pan the monkfish was cooked in. Add the prawns and brown gently, stirring from time to time with a wooden spoon. Pour over the white wine and allow to evaporate. Season with salt and pepper. Then pour in the fish stock, stir and bring slowly to the boil.

Pour the contents of the pan into a liquidizer and leave on maximum speed for a couple of minutes. Strain the mixture into a bowl. Stir in the gelatine, mixing until you are sure it has completely dissolved. Line the bottom and sides of a 2-pint/1-litre rectangular baking pan with foil. Pour in the fish purée and sink the pieces of monkfish into it. Leave to cool at room temperature, then cover with a piece of cling film and refrigerate overnight. Before serving, turn out the mousse on to a dish and garnish as you please. Serve at once.

Cold fish mousse (top) and **stuffed cod**

Salad of Mussels, Bread and Beans

Insalata di Cozze, Pane e Fagioli

To serve 4-5

2¼ lb/1 kg fresh mussels

olive oil

2 large garlic cloves

a little lemon juice

14 oz/400 g tinned haricot beans

2 slices white bread

2 anchovy fillets in oil

1 teaspoon mustard

Worcestershire sauce

2 tablespoons white wine vinegar

fresh chervil or parsley for garnish

Preparation and cooking time: about 45 minutes

Scrape the mussels under cold running water, then put them into a saucepan with a tablespoon of olive oil, a lightly crushed garlic clove and a few drops of lemon juice. Cover and place the pan over a high heat. After a few minutes' cooking and when the mussels have opened, remove them from their shells and leave them to cool in a bowl.

Drain and rinse the beans, then lay them out to dry on a tray covered with a double layer of kitchen paper. Add them to the mussels. Heat 3 tablespoons of oil and the other garlic clove in a frying pan. Fry the bread until it is lightly toasted, then cut it into ¾ inch/2 cm squares. Mix these with the mussels and beans.

Now prepare the dressing: crush the anchovy fillets with a fork in a bowl, then, still mixing with the fork, add the mustard and a dash of Worcestershire sauce, a little salt, 2 tablespoons of vinegar and 5 tablespoons of olive oil. Pour the dressing over the salad, mix once more and garnish with chervil or parsley. Serve immediately.

Prawn and Tomato Salad

Terra-Mare Saporoso

To serve 4-6

¼ pint/150 ml dry white wine

1 bay leaf

2 peppercorns

12 oz/350 g very fresh prawns, unpeeled

2 firm medium tomatoes

2 tablespoons mustard

anchovy paste

juice of ½ lemon

olive oil

a few leaves fresh parsley

Preparation and cooking time: about 30 minutes

Prawn and tomato salad

Heat a saucepan containing about 2 pints/1 litre of water and pour in the wine. Add the bay leaf, peppercorns and salt. Bring gradually to the boil and simmer for about 10 minutes. Meanwhile rinse the prawns thoroughly under cold running water and peel them. Simmer them in the boiling liquid for 5 minutes. Remove with a slotted spoon and lay them to cool on a tray covered with kitchen paper.

Wash the tomatoes, cut them in half horizontally and remove the seeds. Cut the flesh into fairly thin strips. Place the tomatoes and prawns in a salad bowl and prepare the dressing: put 2 tablespoons of mustard in a small bowl together with 4 inches/10 cm of anchovy paste and the strained lemon juice. Mix with a wooden spoon, gradually stirring in 7 tablespoons of olive oil. You should obtain a smooth, creamy sauce. Garnish the salad with parsley and serve the sauce in a sauceboat from which all can help themselves.

Haricot Beans with Tuna

Cannellini Tonnati

To serve 6-8

6 oz/150 g tinned tuna in oil

juice of 1 lemon

1 hard-boiled egg yolk

olive oil

1 lb/500 g tinned haricot beans

1 sprig fresh parsley, coarsely chopped, for garnish

Preparation time: about 20 minutes

Drain the tuna and process it in a blender. Mix the lemon juice and tuna in a bowl. Mash the egg yolk and blend with the tuna. Gradually stir in 3 tablespoons of hot water and 6 tablespoons/100 ml of olive oil to form a smooth, creamy sauce.

Thoroughly drain the beans, place in a serving dish and sprinkle with the chopped parsley. Serve cold with the tuna sauce.

PASTA WITH

Pasta — the dish most associated with Italy — comes in a
bewildering number of shapes and sizes, can be fresh or dried,
and is sometimes coloured with spinach or beetroot, but all
varieties are made from flour bound with eggs or oil, and one
kind can be substituted for another according to taste and
availability. Eaten hot or cold, with a classic sauce or one
made from a variety of seasonal vegetables, pasta is
extremely versatile as either a starter or a main course.

VEGETABLES & CHEESE

Pasta with Fennel
Pasta al Finocchio

To serve 4

1 small onion

2 oz/50 g butter

olive oil

1 large fennel bulb

flour

¼ pint/150 ml stock (or use stock cube)

1 tablespoon fresh cumin leaves, chopped

6 tablespoon/100 ml single cream

12 oz/350 g pasta rings

2 tablespoons grated Pecorino cheese

a little chopped parsley

Preparation and cooking time: about 1 hour

Finely slice the onion and gently fry it in the butter and 2 tablespoons of olive oil. Trim and slice the fennel almost as finely as the onion and add to the pan. Leave for a few minutes, stirring from time to time. Then stir in a teaspoon of flour and the boiling stock. Put in the cumin leaves, stir, cover and cook over a low heat for about 20 minutes. Dilute with more boiling stock if the sauce becomes too dry.

When the fennel is tender, add the cream, stir, add salt and keep the pan over a low heat for a few more seconds.

Cook the pasta in salted boiling water until it is *al dente*. Drain and stir in 2 tablespoons of olive oil. Pour over the fennel sauce and the Pecorino cheese. Mix and serve at once, sprinkled with a little chopped parsley.

Pasta with fennel

Pasta with Turnip Tops
Fettuccia Riccia con Cime di Rapa

To serve 4

2 lb/1 kg turnip tops

4 oz/100 g onion

2 large garlic cloves

olive oil

14 oz/400 g peeled tomatoes

4-5 sprigs fresh coriander

caster sugar

12 oz/350 g scalloped wide pasta noodles (fettuccia)

grated Pecorino cheese

Preparation and cooking time: about 1 hour

Boil a large saucepanful of salted water. Clean and wash the turnip tops and put them in the boiling water for 5-6 minutes. Meanwhile finely chop the onion and 1 garlic clove together and fry in 5 tablespoons of olive oil in a small saucepan. Purée the tomatoes and add to the onion. Season with salt and pepper and add the fresh coriander and a pinch of sugar. Stir and gradually bring to the boil. Turn the heat down low and simmer for about 20 minutes, stirring from time to time.

Remove the turnip tops from the water with a slotted spoon and drain well. Sauté them in a large frying pan in 3 tablespoons of olive oil with 1 lightly crushed garlic clove. Top up the water in the saucepan in which the turnip tops were boiled to make at least 5 pints/3 litres and bring to the boil. Pour in the pasta and cook until it is *al dente*. Drain and put the pasta in the pan with the turnip tops; add the tomato sauce. Sauté for a few minutes then serve with grated Pecorino cheese.

Pink Sauce for Noodles
Sugo Rosa per Fettucine

1 sprig fresh rosemary

1 large garlic clove

¼ pint/150 ml meat gravy, skimmed

¼ pint/150 ml light cream

1 tablespoon tomato ketchup

brandy

6 tinned tomatoes

14 oz/400 g noodles (fettucine)

1 oz/25 g grated Parmesan cheese

1 oz/25 g grated Gruyère cheese

fresh parsley

ground paprika

Chop the rosemary leaves finely with the garlic. Place them in a pan large enough to hold all the pasta, add the gravy and cream and simmer for 5 minutes, stirring frequently. Then add the ketchup, a dash of brandy and the tomatoes, finely chopped. Simmer for about 10 minutes. Cook and drain the pasta, tip it into the sauce, bind with the two cheeses and sprinkle with chopped parsley and a pinch of paprika.

Pasta with Courgettes
Pasta con Zucchini

To serve 4

1 lb/500 g courgettes

1 medium onion

a little parsley

1 large garlic clove

olive oil

½ stock cube

12 oz/350 g fresh pasta

a little grated Parmesan cheese

Preparation and cooking time: 45 minutes

Clean the courgettes and trim them. Wash and dry well, cut them into rounds about ¼ inch/5 mm thick. Finely chop the onion, parsley and garlic and fry in 5 tablespoons of olive oil without browning. Then add the courgettes and crumble in the stock cube. Add a little freshly ground pepper. Cover with boiling water and stir well.

Cover the pan and cook over a moderate heat for about 10 minutes until the courgettes are tender and the liquid has been absorbed. Season to taste. Cook the pasta in salted boiling water until it is *al dente*. Drain and stir in 2 tablespoons of olive oil. Mix in the sauce and serve at once with the Parmesan cheese.

Herb Sauce for Thin Noodles
Sugo di Biete per Trenette

1¾ lb/800 g fresh herbs, basil, thyme, oregano, parsley

olive oil

1 large garlic clove

1-1¼ lb/500 g thin noodles (trenette)

2 oz/50 g grated Emmental cheese

Clean the herbs. Put 6 tablespoons of oil to heat in a small pan with the crushed garlic, and discard the garlic when it has browned. Boil plenty of salted water, add the herbs, cover and bring back to the boil, then add the trenette and cook until *al dente*. Drain the herbs and pasta, dress with the garlic-flavoured oil and the grated Emmental cheese and stir well.

Pasta with courgettes

Delicate Polenta with Mushrooms

Polenta Delicata ai Funghi

To serve 4

1½ pints/900 ml milk

8 oz/250 g corn meal

4 oz/100 g semolina

¾-1 lb/400 g small mushrooms (preferably ceps)

3 oz/75 g butter

flour

ground nutmeg

scant 4 oz/100 g grated Emmental cheese

2 egg yolks

1 garlic clove

a handful of parsley

olive oil

thyme

Preparation and cooking time: about 1 hour

Place on the heat a large saucepan containing 1 pint/500 ml of water and 1½ pints/750 ml of the milk and slowly bring to the boil. Mix the corn meal with the semolina. As soon as the liquids start to boil add the salt and, after a few moments, sprinkle in the mixed corn meal and semolina gradually. At the beginning stir with a small whisk, then with a wooden spoon. Cook the polenta over a medium heat for about 40 minutes, stirring frequently.

In the meantime, clean the mushrooms, trim the stems and wipe the mushrooms with a damp cloth, then cut them into thin slices. In a small saucepan melt 1 oz/25 g of the butter, add the flour and stir with a wooden spoon to prevent lumps forming. Moisten with ¼ pint/150 ml of boiling milk poured in a trickle and, stiring constantly, bring the sauce to the boil.

Remove from the heat, season with salt and ground nutmeg, then stir in the Emmental cheese and 2 egg yolks, stirring vigorously after each addition. Keep the sauce warm in a *bain-marie,* stirring it once in a while.

Finely chop a garlic clove together with a handful of parsley; soften the mixture in 1 oz/25 g of butter and 2 tablespoons of oil, without browning. Add the mushrooms and leave for not more than 5 minutes, seasoning with salt and pepper and a pinch of thyme.

Remove the polenta from the heat and fold in the remaining butter softened and cut in small pieces, then pour it on to a round serving board and make a hollow in the center; pour in the cheese sauce, spread over the mushroom slices and sprinkle with a little chopped parsley. Serve at once.

Pasta Tubes with Broccoli

Sedanini con Broccoletti

To serve 4

1¾ lb/800 g young broccoli

4-6 shallots

a little parsley

2 sprigs fresh fennel

olive oil

12 oz/350 g small pasta tubes

grated Pecorino cheese

Preparation and cooking time: about 30 minutes

Wash the broccoli and divide it into flowerets. Chop the stalks into lengths of about 1½-2 inches/4-5 cm. Cook the broccoli in a saucepan of boiling water for 7-8 minutes. Leave uncovered. While the broccoli is cooking, finely slice the shallots. Chop the parsley and fennel together and sauté with the shallots in 5 tablespoons of olive oil.

Remove the broccoli from the pan with a slotted spoon and, without draining too thoroughly, place it in the frying pan with the other ingredients. Fry the broccoli in turn without mixing – simply shake the pan. Add freshly ground pepper. Into the same water used for the broccoli, there should be at least 5 pints/3 litres, pour the sedanini and boil until the pasta is cooked *al dente*. Drain and sauté in the pan with the broccoli, sprinkling with the Pecorino cheese. Serve at once.

Pasta Shells with Four Cheeses

Lumaconi ai 4 Formaggi

To serve 1

1 oz/25 g Parmesan cheese

1 oz/25 g Sbrinz cheese

1 oz/25 g Emmental cheese

1 oz/25 g Fontina cheese

butter

4 tablespoons/60 ml milk

nutmeg

1 egg yolk

4 oz/100 g pasta shells (lumaconi)

a little chopped parsley for garnish

Preparation and cooking time: about 30 minutes

Grate the Parmesan and Sbrinz cheeses. Cut the Emmental and Fontina cheeses into small cubes and mix these 2 cheeses together well.

In a saucepan melt 1 oz/25 g of butter, without browning; remove the saucepan from the heat and add the 4 cheeses, stirring vigorously with a small wooden spoon. Place the saucepan again over a very low heat (or in a *bain-marie*) and, stirring constantly, melt the cheeses slightly. Then add the warm milk in a trickle, mixing constantly until thoroughly smooth and blended, then season it with a grating of nutmeg. Take off the heat and add a fresh egg yolk. Keep the sauce warm in a *bain-marie,* stirring often.

Cook the pasta in salted boiling water with the pan uncovered, until *al dente.* Drain, pour the cheese "fondue" over it and sprinkle with a pinch of finely chopped parsley. Serve at once before the cheese mixture becomes firm.

Garlic, Oil and Hot Pepper Sauce for Long, Hollow Macaroni

Aglio, Olio e Peperoncino per Fusilli Lunghi Bucati

6 garlic cloves

2 hot chilli peppers

1 lb/500 g hollow macaroni

olive oil

2 oz/50 g grated Parmesan cheese

2 oz/50 g grated Pecorino cheese

Chop the garlic and chilli peppers coarsely and liquidize them with ¼ pint/150 ml of cold water. Add this to a panful of salted hot water, bring to the boil and simmer for 15 minutes, then strain into a second pan. Boil the pasta in this and, when it is cooked *al dente,* drain it and add ⅓ pint/200 ml of olive oil and the two cheeses, stirring well.

Basil Sauce for Pasta Caps

Sugo al Basilico per Orecchiette

5-6 fresh basil leaves

1 garlic clove

2 oz/50 g cooking fat or butter

olive oil

12 oz/350 g pasta caps (orecchiette)

2 tablespoons grated Parmesan cheese

1 tablespoon grated Pecorino cheese

Wash the basil and chop it with the garlic. Heat the fat and 3 tablespoons of olive oil and fry the basil and garlic very gently, adding a generous quantity of freshly ground pepper. Cook and drain the pasta, tip it into the sauce and sprinkle with the two cheeses before serving.

Mushroom Sauce for Fine Noodles

Sugo ai Funghi per Capellini

2 garlic cloves

8 oz/250 g mushrooms

olive oil

2-3 sprigs fresh parsley

¼ pint/150 ml dry white wine

¼ pint/150 ml single cream

1 teaspoon cornflour

3 egg yolks

1 stock cube

4 oz/100 g butter

12 oz/350 g fine noodles (capellini)

2 oz/50 g grated Parmesan cheese

Fry the crushed garlic and the finely sliced mushrooms together in the olive oil, then add the chopped parsley and a little salt. Put the mixture into a blender with the wine, cream, cornflour, egg yolks, stock cube and half the butter, melted. Blend into a smooth sauce, then return it to the pan and simmer for 5 minutes. Serve the fine noodles with this sauce, the rest of the butter in knobs and the grated Parmesan cheese.

Pasta Dumplings with Cheese Sauce

Gnocchi alla Bava

To serve 4

1½ lb/750 g potatoes

6 oz/150 g flour

2 egg yolks

nutmeg

1 oz/25 g Parmesan cheese

2 oz/50 g butter

6 tablespoons/100 ml single cream

Preparation and cooking time: about 30 minutes

Boil the potatoes in salted water, drain, peel and mash them. Add the flour, 1 egg yolk, a little salt and nutmeg. Knead together and divide the dough into small gnocchi shapes. Give them an interesting texture by rolling them on the back of a grater.

Dice the cheese, discarding the rind. Put it in a pan with the melted butter and the cream. Place on a low heat or in a *bain-marie* and stir with a wooden spoon until the cheese has melted. Add the other egg yolk and a generous grinding of pepper and stir briskly.

Cook the gnocchi in plenty of salted boiling water until they rise to the surface. Drain. Pour the sauce over the boiled gnocchi and serve at once.

Small Pasta Dumplings in Egg Sauce

Gnocchietti Sardi in Salsa d'Uova

To serve 8

2 eggs

4 oz/100 g ham

4 oz/100 g mushrooms

2 oz/50 g capers

12 green olives, stoned

5 gherkins, finely sliced

1lb/500 g small pasta dumplings (gnocchi)

2 tablespoons vinegar

olive oil

4 oz/100 g fresh Quartirolo cheese

Preparation and cooking time: about 30 minutes

Hard-boil the eggs and cool them under running water. Cut the ham into tiny cubes, discarding any fat. Place the mushrooms, capers, olives and gherkins in a salad bowl.

Cook the gnocchi in salted boiling water until they rise to the surface, drain well and spread on a tray to cool. Shell the eggs and then finely crumble the yolks into a bowl. Moisten with the vinegar and season with a little salt and pepper. Gradually blend in 2 tablespoons of olive oil.

Place the cold pasta and the diced ham in the salad bowl with the other ingredients. Dress with the prepared sauce and stir well. Dice the fresh Quartirolo cheese and stir it into the salad. Serve.

Cold pasta with ham and olives

Pasta Quills with Yellow Pepper Sauce

Mezze Penne al Peperone

To serve 4

1 large yellow pepper

1 medium onion

olive oil

1 garlic clove

5-6 fresh mint leaves

4 fresh basil leaves

8 oz/250 g skinned tomatoes

½ pint/250 ml light stock (or use a stock cube)

12 oz/350 g small pasta quills (mezze penne)

2 tablespoons grated Pecorino cheese

Preparation and cooking time: 1¼ hours

Grill and peel a ripe, yellow pepper, then cut it into 1 inch/2 cm cubes. Finely slice the onion and soften with the pepper cubes in 5 tablespoons of olive oil, taking care not to brown any of the ingredients. Then add a large garlic clove, with the green core removed, 5-6 leaves of fresh mint and 4 fresh basil leaves, all finely chopped.

Stir, and fry slowly for a few minutes, then pureé the tomatoes and add them. Add the stock and a little salt and pepper and cook in a partly covered pan for about 35 minutes, when the sauce will be just about reduced and well-cooked. Purée half the sauce and return to the pan containing the remainder. Mix well together.

Cook the pasta in salted boiling water until *al dente*. Drain, add a tablespoon of olive oil, then the prepared sauce and the grated Pecorino cheese. Stir and serve.

Pasta with Lentils

Pasta e Lenticche

To serve 6

8 oz/250 g dried lentils

6 oz/150 g potatoes

2 sage leaves

1 large garlic clove

a little parsley

4 oz/100 g peeled tomatoes

olive oil

2 stock cubes

4 oz/100 g pasta shells

3 tablespoons grated Parmesan cheese

Preparation and cooking time: 2½ hours

Pick over the lentils to make sure there are no impurities or grit. Wash under warm running water and place in a saucepan. Peel and dice the potatoes and put these in too. Chop the sage, garlic and parsley and add these too. Purée the tomatoes and add these together with 3 tablespoons of olive oil. Stir and pour in 3½ pints/2 litres of cold water and bring to the boil. Turn the heat down to the minimum as soon as the mixture starts to boil, add the stock cubes, cover and simmer for about 2 hours, stirring from time to time.

When the cooking is completed, purée a ladleful of the mixture and return the purée to the pan.

Stir in and bring back to the boil. Then add the pasta, stir and cook until the pasta is *al dente*. Remove from the heat, add a little freshly milled pepper, 3 tablespoons of olive oil and the Parmesan cheese. Serve, and sprinkle each portion with chopped parsley.

Pasta with yellow pepper sauce

Cold Pasta in Pizzaiola Sauce

Mezze Penne alla Pizzaiola

To serve 8

1 garlic clove

olive oil

about 1¼ lb/600 g tomatoes

8 oz/250 g Mozzarella cheese

1¼ lb/600 g small pasta quills (mezze penne)

a little oil

5 anchovy fillets in oil

2 tablespoons capers

ground oregano

a few fresh basil leaves for garnish

Preparation and cooking time: about 30 minutes

Place the garlic clove in a bowl with 6 tablespoons of olive oil and leave to infuse for a few minutes. Wash and dry the tomatoes and slice them, cutting each slice into 4 pieces. Dice the Mozzarella cheese.

Cook the pasta until *al dente* in salted boiling water. Drain thoroughly and spread out on a tray. Sprinkle with a little oil and leave to cool.

Drain the anchovy fillets and chop them coarsely. When the pasta is cold, place it in a large salad bowl and stir in the pieces of tomato, the cubes of Mozzarella cheese, the chopped anchovy fillets and the capers. Sprinkle with plenty of dried oregano and a pinch of salt. Dress with the oil in which the garlic had been soaking. Stir thoroughly, garnishing with a few leaves of fresh basil and serve.

Pasta and Chick Peas

Pasta e Ceci

To serve 6

4 oz/100 g dried chick peas

1 medium onion

1 large garlic clove

1 small carrot

1 stick celery

8 fresh sorrel leaves

½ sprig of rosemary

4 oz/100 g peeled tomatoes

2 large potatoes, together weighing about 12 oz/350 g

olive oil

2 stock cubes

4 oz/100 g pasta

3 tablespoons grated Parmesan cheese

Preparation and cooking time: 2½ hours plus overnight soaking

Soak the chick peas overnight in cold water. The following day, finely chop the onion with the garlic, carrot and celery together with the sorrel and rosemary leaves. Drain the chick peas and put in a saucepan with all the other ingredients. Chop the tomatoes finely and add these, along with the whole peeled potatoes. Pour in 3½ pints/2 litres of cold water and 3 tablespoons of olive oil. Crumble in the stock cubes and bring to the boil. Then turn the heat down to the minimum, cover the pan and simmer for about 2 hours, stirring from time to time.

Remove the potatoes with a slotted spoon and purée them with about a third of the chick peas, returning the purée to the saucepan. Bring back to the boil and pour in the pasta. Boil over a fairly high heat, keeping the pan uncovered and stirring from time to time. Taste and add salt if required, then stir in 3 tablespoons of olive oil and the Parmesan cheese. Add a little freshly ground pepper. Stir and serve at once.

Cold pasta in pizzaiola sauce

Home-made Agnolotti Pasta with Cep Mushroom Sauce

Agnolotti con Sugo di Porcini

To serve 4-5

2 cabbage leaves

2 small onions

2 oz/50 g butter

olive oil

2 oz/50 g sausage meat

6 oz/175 g cooked beef

4 oz/100 g roast pork

2 oz/50 g grated Parmesan cheese

nutmeg

5 small eggs

12 oz/350 g flour

8 oz/250 g cep mushrooms

1 garlic clove

2-3 sprigs fresh parsley

4 tablespoons dry Marsala wine

½ stock cube

ground thyme

½ pint/300 ml milk

3 tablespoons whipping cream

1 teaspoon cornflour

Preparation and cooking time: about 2 hours

Wash the cabbage leaves thoroughly, then cook in boiling salted water for about 15 minutes. Drain, and when the cabbage has cooled, squeeze out all moisture well. Finely slice 1 onion and fry in 1 oz/25 g butter and 1 tablespoon of olive oil. Add the cabbage leaves and crumble the sausage meat before adding that too. Cook for about 10 minutes, then mince finely with the beef and the pork. Collect the mixture in a bowl and add 4 tablespoons of grated Parmesan cheese, a little salt, pepper and grated nutmeg. Bind with 2 small eggs to a smooth consistency. Taste and adjust the seasoning if necessary.

Prepare the pasta dough from 12 oz/ 350 g of flour and the remaining 3 eggs. Knead energetically until smooth. Roll out the dough a little at a time, keeping the rest beneath an upturned earthenware dish. Cut out 2 inch/5 cm rounds with a pastry cutter. Place a little of the stuffing on one half of each round, then fold over to make semicircular *agnolotti*, pressing down the edges well to seal in the filling. As they are completed, lay them on a lightly floured cloth on a tray. Roll the pastry offcuts into a ball and put this underneath the earthenware dish. When both the pasta dough and the filling are used up, cover with a clean tea towel and leave in a cool place.

Trim the mushrooms, wash them rapidly under running water and drain carefully. Finely chop the remaining onion together with a garlic clove and a handful of parsley and fry in the remaining butter and 2 tablespoons of olive oil, taking care not to brown them. Finely slice the mushrooms and add to the other ingredients. Cook for 3-4 minutes on a fairly high heat, stirring with a wooden spoon. Pour in the Marsala and crumble in half the stock cube. Add a pinch of thyme, stir and when two-thirds of the Marsala has evaporated, pour in the boiling milk. Dissolve the cornflour in the cream and stir that in too. Mix well and simmer for a further few minutes until the sauce has thickened. Cook the *agnolotti* in salted boiling water and when they are cooked, after a few minutes, remove with a slotted spoon. Pour over the sauce and the remaining Parmesan. Mix carefully and serve.

Vegetarian Pasta Salad
Conchiglie Vegetariane

To serve 8

---

4 oz/100 g fresh peas

---

2 baby carrots

---

1 lb/500 g fluted pasta shells

---

4 oz/100 g tinned sweetcorn

---

2 tablespoons mustard

---

juice of ½ lemon

---

olive oil

Preparation and cooking time: about 45 minutes

Heat 2 saucepans of water (one large one and one slightly smaller) and salt them both when they come to the boil.

Cook the fresh shelled peas in the smaller pan, boiling them for about 15 minutes. Drain well, reserving the water, and leave to dry on kitchen paper. Trim and dice the carrots and cook them in the same water for about 12 minutes. Drain and mix with the peas.

Cook the fluted pasta shells in the larger saucepan of boiling water. Drain the pasta when it is cooked *al dente*, and spread it out on a tray to cool.

Drain the sweetcorn and mix it in a salad bowl with the cold peas and carrots. Prepare the dressing: place the mustard, the juice of half a lemon and a pinch of salt and pepper in a bowl. Beat the mixture and blend in 6 tablespoons of olive oil.

Mix the pasta with the vegetables in the salad bowl and dress with the prepared sauce. Stir well and serve.

Vegetarian pasta salad

Tortelloni with Courgettes
Tortelloni di Zucchini

To serve 6

1 lb/500 g courgettes

12 oz/350 g tomatoes

1 oz/30 g plain flour

4 oz/125 g button mushrooms

2 oz/60 g butter

4 oz/125 g grated Parmesan cheese

5 eggs

fresh basil

garlic

dried marjoram

olive oil

nutmeg

Preparation and cooking time: 2 hours

1) Clean and dice the courgettes. Clean and slice the mushrooms. Heat ¼ pint/150 ml of oil in large frying pan with a garlic clove (to be removed before brown). Add the mushrooms and the courgettes and cook for 20 minutes. Allow to cool and then blend them with a food processor. Stir in the Parmesan, 2 egg yolks, a sprinkle of marjoram, a level tablespoon of flour, a sprinkle of nutmeg and salt and pepper.

2) Mix the remaining flour with salt and 3 eggs, and work into a dough. Roll thinly and cut into 2 inch/5 cm strips.

3) Cut the strips into 2 inch/5 cm squares. Put a teaspoon of the courgette mixture onto each square.

4) Fold the tortelloni into triangles, and firmly seal the edges with your fingertips.

5) Peel and dice the tomatoes, melt the butter in a large fry pan and add the tomatoes, salt and 7 chopped basil leaves (or 1 teaspoon dry basil).

6) Cook the sauce for 5 minutes. Meanwhile bring to the boil a large pan of salted water. Drop in the tortelloni. Drain them when still underdone (*al dente*) and add to the sauce. Cook together for a few minutes.

Transfer to a soup tureen and serve hot.

1

2

3

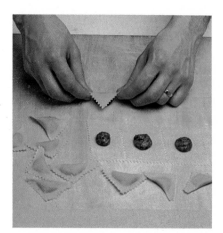

4

5

6

Pasta Ribbons with Mushrooms

Fettuccia Riccia ai Funghi

To serve 1

1 thick slice onion

a few fresh sprigs of parsley

1 garlic clove

butter

1 cep mushroom

1 tablespoon dry Marsala wine

¼ stock cube

½ teaspoon cornflour

milk

4 oz/100 g scalloped pasta ribbons (fettuccia)

Preparation and cooking time: about 30 minutes

Finely chop together the onion, a few parsley sprigs and a small garlic clove. Soften in 1 oz/25 g butter, melted in a small pan. Meanwhile, scrape the dirt from the stem of a very fresh, firm cep mushroom and wash or wipe the cap with a damp cloth. Slice thinly and add the slices to the onion mixture. Sauté for a few minutes, stirring gently with a wooden spoon.

Next, moisten with the dry Marsala wine and season with a quarter of a stock cube. Dissolve half a teaspoon of cornflour in 2 tablespoons of cold milk and add it to the slices of mushroom, stirring with a wooden spoon. Leave the sauce on a very low heat for 4-5 minutes.

Cook the pasta until *al dente* in plenty of salted boiling water. Drain, and pour over the mushrooms sauce to which you have added, at the last moment, half a teaspoon of chopped parsley.

Pasta Riviera-style

Gramigna della Riviera

To serve 4

1 small onion

olive oil

about 8 oz/250 g courgettes

½ stock cube

about 4 oz/100 g ham, in 2 thick slices

12 oz/350 g gramigna pasta

grated Parmesan cheese

chopped fresh parsley

Preparation and cooking time: about 30 minutes

Finely chop the onions and fry gently in 2 tablespoons of olive oil. Top and tail the courgettes, halve lengthwise and then, holding the 2 halves together, slice finely. Add the slices of courgette to the pan, together with half a crumbled stock cube. Lower the heat and cook gently until the courgettes are tender.

Cut the ham into thin strips, discarding any fat. Cook the pasta until *al dente* in plenty of salted boiling water, drain thoroughly and pour into a tureen. Stir in the courgette mixture and the ham, and serve immediately with cheese. Top with chopped parsley.

Ligurian-style Butterfly Pasta

Farfallette alla Ligure

To serve 4

4 oz/100 g small tender borage leaves

4 medium artichokes

1 medium onion

a little parsley

1 large garlic clove

olive oil

¼ pint/150 ml stock (or use stock cube)

1 sprig fresh thyme

12 oz/350 g small pasta butterflies (farfallette)

a handful of grated Peccorino cheese

Preparation and cooking time: 45 minutes

Wash and drain the borage, then coarsely chop. Clean the artichokes, keeping the leaves, cut them in half and then in thin slices. Chop the onions together with the garlic and parsley and sauté in 5 tablespoons of olive oil in a pan. Add the artichokes and borage, stir and fry gently for a few seconds. Boil the stock and pour this into the pan. Flavour with a pinch of thyme and a little freshly milled pepper.

Cover the pan and simmer for about 20 minutes over a moderate heat, until the artichokes are tender and have absorbed all the liquid. Taste and adjust the seasoning. Cook the pasta until it is *al dente* in plenty of salted boiling water. Drain and stir in 2 tablespoons of olive oil, serve with the artichoke and borage sauce and with the grated Peccorino cheese.

Toasted Flour Sauce for Macaroni

Condimento di Farina Tostata per Maccheroni

1 heaped tablespoon flour

2 heaped tablespoons grated Parmesan cheese

1 large onion

4 oz/100 g butter

12 oz/350 g macaroni

Pre-heat the oven to 325°F/170°C/gas mark 3. Put the flour on a small baking tray and brown it in the oven. Spread it out on a plate and add the cheese and some pepper. Chop the onion finely and fry it in the butter in a covered pan over a low heat, so the onion becomes slightly golden. Cook and drain the pasta, sprinkle with the flour mixture and then pour on the butter and onion.

Thin Noodles with Basil Sauce

Trenette al Pesto

To serve 4

2 garlic cloves

2 teaspoons pine-nuts

about 18 fresh basil leaves

½ oz/10 g Pecorino cheese

½ oz/10 g grated Parmesan cheese

olive oil

2oz/50 g fresh French beans

1 potato

12 oz/350 g thin noodles (trenette)

Preparation and cooking time: about 45 minutes

Pre-heat the oven to 350°F/180°C/gas mark 4. Chop the garlic and place in a mortar with a little salt. Lightly toast the pine-nuts in the oven for 3-4 minutes and leave to cool. Wash and dry the basil leaves and add them one at a time to the mortar, alternating them with a few pine-nuts. Pound with a pestle, gradually adding the grated cheeses. Continue pounding until the ingredients have blended to form a green paste. Transfer the mixture to a bowl and gradually stir in enough olive oil to form a smooth paste.

Top and tail the beans and cut them into small pieces. Dice the potato. Cook the beans for 10 minutes in plenty of salted boiling water. Add the diced potato and the pasta. Cook the pasta until *al dente* and drain it, reserving 2 tablespoons of the cooking liquid to dilute the basil sauce. Dress the pasta with the basil sauce, stir well and serve with more grated Parmesan cheese.

PASTA WITH

Italians eat some kind of pasta almost every day and cook it *al dente*, just to the point where you can feel your teeth biting into it. Pasta can be eaten with a traditional sauce, such as Bolognese or *alle vongole*, or with a more adventurous choice of seafood or meat accompaniment.

SEAFOOD & MEAT

Green and White Noodles with Bolognese Sauce

Paglia e Fieno con Ragú Pasquale

To serve 6

1 medium onion

1 large garlic clove

½ sprig rosemary

1 small bunch parsley

1 stalk celery

2 small carrots

butter

olive oil

4 oz/100 g beef

4 oz/100 g lamb

4 oz/100 g sausage meat

2 slices bacon

6 tablespoons/100 ml dry white wine

1 oz/25 g flour

12 oz/350 g tomatoes

1 stock cube

4 oz/100 g young peas

1 lb/500 g green and white noodles (tagliatelle)

1 oz/25 g grated Parmesan cheese

Preparation and cooking time: about 2 hours

Finely chop the onion with a large garlic clove, the leaves of half a sprig of rosemary and a small bunch of parsley. Dice the celery and carrot. Put these ingredients into a saucepan with 1 oz/25 g butter and 3 tablespoons of oil. Soften but do not allow to brown.

Meanwhile, mince the beef, lamb and sausage meat and dice the bacon. Add to the vegetables in the pan, stir and brown slightly. Then pour the white wine in and allow to evaporate almost completely. Sprinkle in a level tablespoon of flour.

Stir well to prevent lumps forming.

Purée the tomatoes and add immediately after the flour together with a pint/500 ml of cold water, the crumbled stock cube and some freshly ground black pepper. Stir and bring to the boil, then turn the heat down to simmer, cover the pan and cook for about 1½ hours. Stir occasionally and dilute with a little boiling water if necessary.

Parboil the peas and add them 15 minutes before cooking is completed. Cook the pasta until *al dente* in plenty of salted boiling water. Drain and mix in 2 tablespoons of olive oil, then serve with the sauce and the grated Parmesan cheese.

Bacon Sauce for Ridged Macaroni

Sugo Affumicato per Mezze Maniche Rigate

1 large onion

olive oil

8 oz/250 g smoked bacon

1 lb/500 g tomatoes

1 lb/500 g ridged macaroni (mezze maniche rigate)

Chop the onion finely and sweat it in a pan with 2 tablespoons of olive oil without browning. Cut the bacon into short strips ½ inch/1 cm wide and add it to the softened onion. Purée the chopped tomatoes and add them, with salt and pepper to taste. Stir, put the lid on and cook for about 20 minutes, then pour over the pasta, cooked until *al dente*.

Milk Sauce for Thin Spaghetti

Salsa al Latte per Spaghettini

1 small onion

butter

6 oz/150 g smoked bacon

2 egg yolks

cornflour

scant ½ pint/250 ml milk

3 oz/75 g grated Parmesan cheese

1-2 sprigs fresh parsley

14 oz/400 g thin spaghetti (spaghettini)

Slice the onion finely, place it in a large pan with 1 oz/25 g of butter and sweat it gently, taking care it does not brown. Cut the bacon into short narrow strips, add it to the onion and cook until it becomes transparent. Beat the egg yolks with a large pinch of cornflour, gradually add the milk, then half the cheese and the chopped parsley, and season with salt and pepper. Add this to the bacon and onion and bring to the boil. Cook and drain the pasta and tip it into the pan with the sauce. Before serving, sprinkle with the remaining grated Parmesan cheese.

Noodles with Bolognese sauce

Home-made Cannelloni in Cream Sauce

Cannelloni Ripieni in Bianco

To serve 10

1 small onion

1 carrot

1 stalk celery

1 bay leaf

half a chicken, weighing about 1¼ lb/600 g

4 chicken livers

1 stale bread roll

4 oz/100 g ham

6 oz/150 g butter

about 3 tablespoons dry Marsala wine

8 tablespoons grated Parmesan cheese

6 eggs

14 oz/400 g flour

olive oil

⅓ pint/200 ml light cream

Preparation and cooking time: about 3½ hours

Bring about 2 pints/1 litre of water to the boil in a saucepan and add a little salt, half the onion, the carrot, the celery rib, bay leaf and chicken. Cover the pan and cook on a moderate heat for about 1 hour.

Trim and wash the livers.

Crumble the roll and soften it with some of the cooking liquid from the chicken. Finely chop the fat of the ham and the remaining half onion.

Place the chopped onion and ham fat in a small frying pan with a large knob of butter and cook on a very low heat for a few minutes. Add the chicken livers and cook for a further 10 minutes, occasionally pouring on a little Marsala. Remove from the heat.

Remove the chicken with a slotted spoon and allow it to cool slightly. Strain the stock. Bone the chicken and mince the meat finely in a liquidizer with the chicken livers and ham. Place the mixture in a bowl and stir in 4 tablespoons of grated Parmesan cheese, the drained bread and 3 of the eggs. Season to taste.

Prepare the pasta: sift 12 oz/350 g of flour into a bowl and make a well in the centre. Place 3 eggs and a tablespoon of olive oil in the well and hand mix with the flour to form a firm dough, kneading for about 10 minutes. Roll out thinly.

Heat plenty of water in a large saucepan. Coat the rolled-out dough in flour, roll it up and cut it into pieces about 4 inches/10 cm wide. Unroll the strips and cut them into 4 inch/10 cm lengths. Once the water has come back to the boil, add salt and a tablespoon of olive oil. Put the squares of pasta in the water one at a time. As soon as the water comes back to the boil, drain the pasta and spread it out on a tea-towel to dry.

Place some of the prepared filling on each square of pasta and then roll them up on a greased baking tray.

Pre-heat the oven to 400°F/200°C/gas mark 6. Melt 2 oz/50 g of butter in a saucepan and blend in 2 oz/50 g of flour to form a smooth *roux*. Pour in 1 pint/500 ml of the strained chicken stock, stirring constantly. Bring to the boil, blend in the cream and season to taste.

Cover the cannelloni with the prepared sauce and dot with about 2 oz/50 g of butter, cut into small pieces. Sprinkle with the rest of the grated Parmesan cheese and bake in the oven for about 15 minutes. Serve.

Peppery Sauce for Noodles

Salsa Peverada per Tagliatelle

4 oz/100 g chicken livers

4 oz/100 g calves' liver

1 onion

4-5 sprigs fresh parsley

4 oz/100 g smoked bacon

2 oz/50 g capers

rind of ½ lemon

olive oil

6 anchovy fillets

2 garlic cloves

6 tablespoons/100 ml red wine

1 lb/500 g noodles (tagliatelle)

Mince or chop the livers and reserve them. Chop the onion, parsley, bacon, capers and lemon rind together. Heat 3 tablespoons of olive oil and add the chopped anchovies and the garlic. When the garlic is golden, remove and discard it. Add the chopped onion and bacon mixture to the pan. As soon as it is browned, pour in the red wine and add the livers. Cook over a high heat for 5 minutes and season with freshly ground black pepper. Cook and drain the pasta and serve with the sauce.

Devilled Sauce for Pasta Dumplings

Sugo alla Diavola per Malloreddus

4 Italian poaching sausages

¼ pint/150 ml dry white wine

4 oz/100 g peas

2 sprigs fresh rosemary

1 small piece hot chilli pepper

2 oz/50 g butter

2 tablespoons vinegar

12 oz/350 g pasta dumplings (gnocchi)

2 oz/50 g grated Parmesan cheese

2 oz/50 g grated Pecorino cheese

Wash the sausages, place in a small pan with ¼ pint/150 ml of water and the wine, cover and cook for about 20 minutes. Skin and dice them and return them to the pan with the same liquid, add the peas, season with salt and pepper and cook for about 15 minutes, stirring occasionally.

Finely chop the rosemary leaves. Melt the butter in a large pan, gently fry the rosemary, then add the vinegar and the sausages and peas with their liquid. Toss the cooked gnocchi in this sauce, adding the ground chilli pepper and the two cheeses.

Pasta Twists with Pork Ragout

Fusilli con Ragú du Lonza

To serve 4

½ small onion

butter

olive oil

8 oz/250 g pork loin

6 tablespoons/100 ml dry white wine

1 stock cube

½ sachet saffron

12 oz/350 g pasta twists (fusilli)

1 teaspoon cornflour

6 tablespoons/100 ml milk

15 capers in vinegar

Worcestershire sauce

Preparation and cooking time: about 40 minutes

Chop the onion and soften it in 1 oz/25g butter and 1 tablespoon of oil. Cut the meat into small cubes and brown them quickly in the pan, then moisten with the white wine, let it evaporate, then season with the crumbled stock cube. Cook the pasta until *al dente* in plenty of salted boiling water flavoured with saffron.

Dissolve the cornstarch in the cold milk and add to the ragout together with the well-drained capers. Season with a dash of Worcestershire sauce, stir and remove from the heat. Drain the pasta, place it in a warmed bowl and pour over it a few drops of oil and then the ragout sauce. Serve at once.

You can use other types of short pasta for this dish such as penne, rigatoni, sedani, farfalle and so on. The Worcestershire sauce is important and, should you not have any, substitute a bit of anchovy paste and white pepper.

Pasta twists with pork ragout

Creamy Fluted Macaroni

Penne 'due Torri'

To serve 4

2 oz/50 g mortadella sausage

2 oz/50 g slice ham

1 small onion, thinly sliced

1 garlic clove

butter

olive oil

6 tablespoons/100 ml dry white wine

1 teaspoon cornflour

1 pint/500 ml light stock (or use stock cube)

Worcestershire sauce

12 oz/350 g fluted macaroni

6 tablespoons/100 ml single cream

2 tablespoons grated Parmesan cheese

2 tablespoons chopped fresh parsley

Preparation and cooking time: about 40 minutes

Cut the mortadella and ham into ¼ inch/5 mm cubes. Gently fry the onion and a crushed garlic clove in 1 oz/25 g of butter and 2 tablespoons of olive oil until transparent. Add the cubes of mortadella and ham and cook for a few minutes. Pour on the wine and allow it to evaporate almost completely. Dissolve the cornflour in 3 tablespoons of cold water and add it to the pan, together with the boiling stock and a splash of Worcestershire sauce. Stir and simmer gently until the liquid has reduced by two-thirds to form a creamy sauce.

Cook the pasta until *al dente* in salted boiling water, drain it and stir it into the prepared sauce. Blend in the cream. Remove the pan from the heat and stir in the grated Parmesan cheese and chopped parsley. Serve .

Cream Sauce for Fluted Macaroni

Salsa alla Crema per Pipe Rigate

2 oz/50 g ham

3 tablespoons/100 ml single cream

2 egg yolks

3 oz/75 g butter

1 oz/25 g grated Parmesan cheese

12 oz/350 g fluted macaroni (pipe rigate)

Chop the ham finely and place it in the serving bowl. Warm the cream, take it off the heat, incorporate the egg yolks and add it to the ham. Flake the butter and stir it into the other ingredients with the grated Parmesan cheese and freshly ground pepper. Cook and drain the pasta and stir it into the prepared sauce.

Creamy fluted macaroni

Pasta Thimbles with Sausage and Carrot

Ditali Rigati con Salsiccia e Carota

To serve 4-5

4 oz/100 g carrots

1 celery heart

4 oz/100 g onion

butter

olive oil

8 oz/250 g sausages

½ stock cube

6 tablespoons/100 ml dry rosé wine

12 oz/350 g fluted pasta thimbles

grated Parmesan cheese

Preparation and cooking time: about 1 hour

Clean the carrot and celery then cube them and cook for about 15 minutes in boiling salted water. Finely chop the onion and soften it in 1 oz/25 g of butter, melted together with 2 tablespoons of oil. Skin the sausages and mash the meat with a fork. Add to the lightly-fried onion, season with the half crumbled stock cube and moisten with the rosé wine. When the wine has evaporated completely, add the drained cubed vegetables and remove from the heat.

Meanwhile cook the pasta in plenty of salted boiling water until *al dente*. Drain it and pour the sausage and vegetable sauce over it then pour into a warmed tureen and serve with cheese.

Orecchiette with Würstchen

Orecchiette with Würstchen

Orecchiette Nord-Sud

To serve 4

a bunch of parsley

3 large boiling sausages

12 oz/350 g orecchiette pasta

butter

olive oil

1 tablespoon cornflour

6 tablespoons/100 ml milk

½ stock cube

grated Pecorino cheese

Preparation and cooking time: about 20 minutes

Wash and dry the parsley, then coarsely chop together with the sausages, first cut up into smaller pieces. Cook the pasta in salted boiling water until it is *al dente*.

Melt 1 oz/25 g butter in a large frying pan together with 5 tablespoons of olive oil. When the fat is hot, add the parsley and sausage. Dissolve the cornflour in a little cold water and stir this into the mixture in the frying pan. Then pour in the cold milk and flavour with the stock cube.

Cook until the sauce is smooth and thick. Drain the pasta and pour it into the frying pan off the heat. Mix carefully, then pour the contents of the frying pan into a warmed soup tureen and serve at once with the Pecorino cheese sprinkled on top.

Orecchiette with Tomato and Sausage Ragout

Orecchiette con Pomodoro e Salsiccia

To serve 4-5

1 small onion

1 stick celery

1 small carrot

2 oz/50 g bacon

3 oz/75 g butter

1 garlic clove

1 sprig basil

3-4 sprigs parsley

4 oz/100 g skinned sausages

6 tablespoons/100 ml dry white wine

flour

1 lb/500 g ripe tomatoes

14 oz/400 g orecchiette pasta

olive oil

4 tablespoons mild Pecorino cheese, grated

Preparation and cooking time: about 2 hours

Finely chop together the onion, celery and carrot and fry with the diced bacon in the butter in a small saucepan. Add a large garlic clove (to be removed and thrown away later), a sprig of basil and 3-4 sprigs of parsley, tied in a small bunch. Add the sausage meat mashed with a fork. Moisten with the wine and let it evaporate almost completely. Then sprinkle with a teaspoon of flour. Chop the tomatoes and purée them. Add them to the pan. Stir, salt and pepper lightly and cook over a very low heat for about 1½ hours, moistening when the sauce becomes too thick with a small amount of hot water or stock.

About 30 minutes before the ragout is ready cook the pasta until *al dente* in plenty of salted boiling water. Drain the orecchiette and mix immediately with 3 tablespoons of olive oil. Add the ragout, discarding the garlic and the small bunch of seasoning herbs. Sprinkle with the Pecorino cheese, mix once more and serve.

Curry Sauce for Hollow Spaghetti

Salsa al Curry per Bucatini

2 large onions

4 oz/100 g smoked bacon

2 oz/50 g butter

olive oil

Marsala, port or Madeira wine

½ stock cube

1 teaspoon curry powder

12 oz/350 g hollow spaghetti (bucatini)

Slice the onion finely and dice the bacon. Melt the butter with 3 tablespoons of oil in a wide pan, add the onion and bacon and lightly brown them. Pour in the wine, stirring with a wooden spoon, then lower the heat and simmer for about 10 minutes. Stir from time to time, gradually adding the crumbled half stock cube and the curry powder. Cook and drain the pasta, tip it into the sauce, stir and serve.

Spaghetti with Frankfurters and Olives

Spaghetti con Würstel e Olive

To serve 4

1 medium onion, chopped

butter

olive oil

4 skinless frankfurter sausages, sliced

brandy

8 green olives, stoned and sliced

½ stock cube

cornflour

12 oz/350 g spaghetti

1 oz/25 g grated Parmesan cheese

Preparation and cooking time: about 30 minutes

Sauté the onion in a large knob of butter and 2 tablespoons of olive oil. Add the slices of frankfurter sausage and cook for a few minutes. Sprinkle generously with brandy and flambé. Add the olives and cook for a further 2-3 minutes.

Pour on about ¼ pint/150 ml of boiling water and add the crumbled half stock cube. Dissolve a large pinch of cornflour in 2 tablespoons of cold water and pour into the pan, stirring constantly. Simmer for 10 minutes.

Cook the spaghetti in plenty of salted boiling water, drain and cover with the sauce. Sprinkle with cheese and serve.

Pasta with Tuna and Peppers

'Sedani' al Tonno e Peperone

To serve 4

1 small onion

olive oil

1 red pepper weighing about 12 oz/350 g

4 oz/100 g tinned tuna

12 oz/350 g short macaroni

⅓ pint/200 ml tomato sauce

1 stock cube

1 sprig fresh parsley

a little grated Pecorino cheese

Preparation and cooking time: about 25 minutes

Finely chop the onion and fry gently in 3 tablespoons of olive oil until transparent. Meanwhile wash the pepper and cut it in half, discarding the stalk and seeds. Cut it into short, thick strips and add them to the onion and cook for a few minutes.

Drain the tuna, break it into pieces with a fork and add it to the pan. Cook the pasta until *al dente* in plenty of salted boiling water. Add the tomato sauce and the crumbled stock cube to the tuna mixture and cook on a low heat.

Drain the pasta, pour it into a tureen and dress with the prepared sauce. Top with chopped parsley and serve immediately with the grated Pecorino cheese.

Tagliatelle with Salmon

Tagliatelle Emiliane al Salmone

To serve 1

1 thick slice red onion

1 garlic clove

1 oz/25 g butter

2 oz/50 g canned salmon

1 teaspoon tomato paste

4 tablespoons/60 ml milk

1 teaspoon cornflour

4 oz/100 g noodles (tagliatelle)

1-2 slices smoked salmon

Preparation and cooking time: about 30 minutes

Finely chop the red onion and garlic together, then melt 1 oz/25 g of the butter in a pan without browning. Sauté the chopped mixture without browning, stirring occasionally with a wooden spoon. Next add the salmon, first drained and with any skin and bones removed, and break into small pieces with a fork. Add a teaspoon of tomato paste, stir and cook for a few moments. Meanwhile, dissolve a teaspoon of cornflour in the cold milk, then pour it over the salmon and, stirring constantly, bring to the boil. Season with pepper and remove from the heat.

Cook the pasta until *al dente* in plenty of salted boiling water. Meanwhile cut the smoked salmon into short strips. Drain the pasta and pour over the prepared sauce. Garnish with the strips of salmon and with remaining butter cut in small pieces. Serve at once.

Tagliatelle with salmon

Corsair Sauce for Pasta Quills

Sugo alla Corsara per Penne Rigate

1-1¼ lb/500 g razor-clams

olive oil

6 tablespoons/100 ml dry white wine

2 garlic cloves

a small piece chilli pepper

4-5 sprigs fresh parsley

a few fresh basil leaves

1 stock cube

4 large ripe tomatoes

12 oz/350 g cups fluted pasta quills (penne)

3 oz/75 g grated Pecorino cheese

Wash the clams well and put them in a frying pan with 3 tablespoons of olive oil, the wine and the finely chopped garlic, chilli pepper, parsley and basil. Add the stock cube, dissolved in hot water, and simmer for 10 minutes.

Remove the opened clams from their shells, and cut each one into three. Scald the tomatoes, remove the skins and seeds and cut the flesh into strips. Strain the clam liquid into a large pan, add the tomatoes and clams and toss the cooked pasta in it. Sprinkle with the grated Pecorino cheese.

Angler's Sauce for Vermicelli

Sugo alla Pescatora per Vermicelli

2½ lb/1.2 kg mussels

olive oil

1 onion

1 garlic clove

2 firm, ripe tomatoes

½ teaspoon anchovy paste

2-3 sprigs fresh parsley

a few fresh basil leaves

12 oz/350 g vermicelli

Wash the mussels well, heat them in a covered skillet with a little olive oil and take them out of their shells when they open. Chop the onion and garlic and sweat them in 3 tablespoons of olive oil. Scald, peel and de-seed the tomatoes, chop them and add to the onion with the mussels, anchovy paste, freshly ground pepper and a little salt. Chop the parsley and basil finely. Cook and drain the pasta and serve it with the sauce, sprinkled with the chopped herbs, 3 or 4 tablespoons of olive oil and a final seasoning of black pepper.

Oriental Sauce for Pasta Tubes

Sogo all'Orientale per Sedanini Rigati

1 medium onion

1 garlic clove

4-5 sprigs fresh parsley

olive oil

6 oz/150 g tinned tuna

12 anchovy fillets in oil

12 oz/350 g fluted pasta tubes (sedanini rigati)

½ stock cube

1 teaspoon soy sauce

grated Parmesan cheese

Chop the onion, garlic and parsley finely together. Sweat the mixture in 6 tablespoons of olive oil, then add the tuna and anchovies. Fry gently, using a fork to break up the fish. Cook and drain the pasta when it is al dente and tip it into the pan with the sauce, keeping the heat fairly high. Dissolve the stock cube and soy sauce in ¼ pint/150 ml of the pasta cooking water, add this and let it soak in for a couple of minutes. Serve sprinkled with plenty of grated Parmesan cheese.

Seafood Pasta Twists
Fusilli "Marechiaro"

To serve 6

1¼ lb/600 g firm, ripe tomatoes

1 medium onion

1 garlic clove

1 small green pepper

olive oil

4 oz/100 g cooked mussels

6 fresh basil leaves

a little sugar

1¼ lb/600 g pasta twists (fusilli)

1 sprig fresh parsley

Preparation and cooking time: about 1 hour

Remove the stalks from the tomatoes, wash, dry and purée them. Chop the onion finely with the garlic and pepper and sauté the mixture gently in olive oil, taking care not to let it brown. Add the drained mussels, giving them a few moments to absorb the flavours, then add the tomatoes and the torn-up basil leaves. Salt lightly, then add the pepper and a good pinch of sugar. Stir and simmer for 30 minutes over a moderate heat with the lid half on.

Cook the pasta until *al dente* in plenty of salted boiing water. Drain, and add the prepared sauce plus 3 tablespoons of olive oil and a little more pepper. Stir carefully, turn into a heated tureen, sprinkle with chopped parsley and serve.

Cold Pasta Twists with Salmon and Asparagus

Fusilli al Salmone e Asparagi

To serve 8

½ lb/250 g smoked salmon, cut in thin strips

3 tablespoons pistachio nuts

½ lb/250 g tinned asparagus

1 lb/500 g pasta twists

large lemon

Preparation and cooking time: about 30 minutes

Pre-heat the oven to 425°F/220°C/gas mark 7. Parboil the pistachio nuts in a little salted water and then rub off their skins. Place the nuts on a baking tray and toast them lightly in the oven for 3-4 minutes. Drain the asparagus, trim and cut into ½ inch/1 cm lengths.

Cook the pasta until *al dente* in plenty of salted boiling water. Drain thoroughly and spread on a tray to cool.

Strain the juice of a large lemon into a bowl and add a pinch of salt and pepper. Stir in 6 tablespoons olive oil.

Place the cold pasta in a salad bowl, add the strips of salmon, the pieces of asparagus and the chopped nuts. Pour on the dressing, stir and serve.

Pasta Tubes with Crab Meat

Rigatoni al Granchio

To serve 1

small shallot

1 small piece celery heart

butter

olive oil

2 oz/50 g crab meat

2 tablespoons sparkling white wine

1 tablespoon tomato paste

2-3 tablespoons concentrated fish stock

4 oz/100 g large fluted pasta tubes (rigatoni)

Preparation and cooking time: about 30 minutes

Finely chop together the shallot and celery heart and sauté, without browning, in 1 oz/25 g of butter melted in a frying pan with a teaspoon of olive oil. Meanwhile, drain the crab meat, removing any cartilage, and shred finely before adding to the pan. Cook for a few minutes, stirring.

Next, moisten the crab with a sprinkling of sparkling wine and let it evaporate almost completely, keeping the heat low and stirring often. Then add the tomato paste and 2 tablespoons of fish stock. Stir once more and leave the sauce to simmer for 5-7 minutes. If it dries out too much, moisten with another tablespoon of fish stock. Season with salt and white pepper.

Cook the pasta until *al dente* in plenty of salted boiling water. Drain, remove to a warmed plate and pour the hot crab sauce over it. Garnish, if you like, with celery leaves. Serve at once.

Cold pasta twists with salmon and asparagus

Mascarpone Sauce for Thin Noodles

Sugo al Mascarpone per Tagliolini

4 oz/100 g raw ham

6 oz/150 g Mascarpone cheese

1 tablespoon Worcestershire sauce

12 oz/350 g thin noodles (tagliolini)

1 oz/25 g grated Parmesan cheese

1 oz/25 g grated Gruyère cheese

Cut the ham into fine strips. Warm the Mascarpone in a wide saucepan with the Worcestershire sauce and the ham over a low heat, stirring with a wooden spoon. Boil the noodles in salted water until *al dente,* drain them, tip them into the sauce, add the grated cheeses, stir and serve at once.

Pasta tubes with crab meat *(left)*

Pasta Ribbons with Piquant Tuna Fish Sauce

Fettuccine Ricce al Tonno

To serve 4-5

½ small onion

1 garlic clove

1 sprig parsley

olive oil

6 oz/175 g tinned tuna in oil

butter

1 oz/25 g flour

½ pint/300 ml stock (or use 1 stock cube)

white pepper

1 small pimiento in vinegar

10 capers in vinegar

12 oz/350 g scalloped pasta ribbons (fettuccine)

Preparation and cooking time: about 40 minutes

Chop the onion with 1 garlic clove and a parsley sprig. Lightly fry them in 3 tablespoons of olive oil in a small pan without browning. When the onion is softened, drain the tuna and mash it roughly with a fork, then add it to the lightly fried mixture and leave on the heat for a few more minutes.

Prepare a smooth béchamel sauce by melting 1 oz/25 g of butter in another pan, stirring in the flour and adding the hot stock; season with a grinding of white pepper. Mix the sauce with the tuna mixture and keep the sauce warm in a hot *bain-marie.* Roughly chop the drained pimiento and the drained capers and then add them to the sauce. Cook the pasta in salted boiling water until *al dente.* Drain well and pour the tuna sauce over it. Pour the pasta into a large warmed tureen or serving dish and serve.

The pasta suggested is the one which is most suited to this type of sauce; however, you can also obtain excellent results by using other kinds of wide egg noodles.

Pasta ribbons with piquant tuna sauce

Hollow Spaghetti with Caviar

Bucatini al Caviale

To serve 1

small piece onion

½ garlic clove

olive oil

2 oz/50 g caviar

a little vodka

3 tablespoons fish stock

Worcestershire sauce

2 tablespoons single cream

4 oz/100 g hollow spaghetti (bucatini)

fresh basil for garnish

Preparation and cooking time: about 30 minutes

Finely chop together the onion and half garlic clove. Soften in a pan with 2 tablespoons of olive oil, without browning. Next add the caviar and let it heat for a few moments, without frying; stir with a wooden spoon.

Moisten with a sprinkling of vodka and let it evaporate almost completely, keeping the heat very low. Pour in the hot fish stock, letting it reduce almost entirely before adding a sprinkling of Worcestershire sauce and, off the heat, 2 tablespoons of cream. Mix gently and keep the sauce warm in a *bain-marie*.

Cook the pasta until *al dente* in plenty of salted boiling water. Drain and season, first with a tablespoon of olive oil, then with the caviar sauce. Garnish the dish with fresh basil and serve immediately.

Pasta Salad 'in Evening Dress'

Gramigna in Abito da Sera

To serve 8

1 egg

5 tablespoons olive paste

about 2 oz/50 g lumpfish roe

1 lb/500 g gramigna pasta

a little oil

olive oil

Preparation and cooking time: about 20 minutes

Hard-boil the egg and cool it under running water. Shell the egg and take out the yolk. Place the black olive paste and the lumpfish roe in a salad bowl.

Cook the pasta in plenty of salted boiling water until slightly *al dente*. Drain well and spread out on a tray. Sprinkle with a little oil and leave to cool.

Pour the cold pasta into the salad bowl and stir in the olive paste and lumpfish roe. Dress with 5 tablespoons of olive oil and stir well. Finely crumble the egg yolk on to the pasta and top with a little lumpfish roe. Stir in the crumbled yolk and lumpfish roe at the table just before serving the pasta.

Thin Noodles with Clams

Linguine alle Vongole

To serve 4

1 garlic clove

olive oil

1 small onion, finely chopped

8 oz/250 g frozen clams

12 oz/350 g clam sauce

4 oz/100 g frozen peas

1 stock cube

12 oz/350 g thin noodles (linguine)

Preparation and cooking time: about 20 minutes

Sauté the whole garlic clove in 4 tablespoons of olive oil. Discard the garlic and add the finely chopped onions to the pan. Fry them gently. Place the clams in the pan and allow to defrost on a low heat. Add the clam sauce and the peas. Stir in the crumbled stock cube and simmer on a moderate heat.

Cook the pasta until *al dente*, in salted boiling water, drain and pour into a warmed tureen. Dress with the prepared sauce and serve immediately.

Hollow spaghetti with caviar

Pasta Butterflies with Chicken and Prawn Sauce

Farfalle con Pollo e Gamberetti

To serve 1

½ small onion

butter

small chicken breast

few shelled prawns

1 tablespoon cognac

2 tablespoons dry white wine

6 tablespoons/100 ml chicken stock

½ teaspoon cornflour

4 tablespoons single cream

4 oz/100 g pasta butterflies (farfalle)

1 sprig parsley and 1 prawn for garnish

Preparation and cooking time: about 40 minutes

Finely chop the onion and soften it gently, without browning, in 1 oz/25 g butter. Meanwhile, finely mince the trimmed chicken breast and prawns. Add them to the onion and let them cook over a low heat, stirring frequently with a wooden spoon. Then moisten with the cognac and, when it has evaporated almost entirely, pour in the white wine.

When the wine has been absorbed almost completely, pour in the cold chicken stock, in which you have dissolved half a teaspoon of cornflour, and the cream. Stir and simmer gently on a very low heat for a few minutes, then liquidize in the blender to obtain a smooth and creamy sauce. Season with pepper, adjust the salt to taste and keep it warm in a *bain-marie*.

Heat 2 pints/1 litre of water in a saucepan and salt it when it starts to boil. Plunge in the pasta and cook until *al dente*. Drain and pour over the chicken and prawn sauce. If you like, garnish with a sprig of parsley and a prawn. Serve at once.

Thin noodles with clams

Pasta butterflies with chicken and prawn sauce

PIZZA

The term pizza means a "pie" and throughout Italy a variety of open yeast pastry pies are traditional and much enjoyed. Here are recipes for a crispy, light Pizza Napoletana, a Roman-style pizza with mozzarella, and *calzone* made from pizza dough. You can also experiment with your own toppings, using whatever is in your larder.

Egg Pizza
Pizza all'Uovo

To serve 4

flour

1 lb/500 g pizza dough

olive oil

¾ lb/400 g firm, ripe tomatoes

oregano

1 medium courgette

4 oz/100 g Mozzarella cheese

slice lean ham

a few fennel leaves

2 tablespoons grated mild Pecorino cheese

1 egg

Preparation and cooking time: about 45 minutes plus any defrosting time

Pre-heat the oven to 400°F/200°C/gas mark 6. Flour a pastry-board and roll the dough, defrosted if necessary, into a ball, then flatten it out to a round about 12 inches/30 cm in diameter. Lightly grease a baking tray and place the dough on it. With your fingertips, press down the dough just inside the edge all the way round to give it a raised edge.

Blanch the tomatoes in boiling salted water for a few seconds and skin them. Cut them in half, remove the seeds, then chop them coarsely. Season them with salt, pepper and a pinch of oregano. Trim and finely slice the courgette. Bring the water in which the tomatoes were blanched back to the boil and put in the courgette slices for a bare 2 minutes. Remove them with a slotted spoon and drain carefully. Lay them out to dry on a large plate covered with a double layer of kitchen paper. Dice the Mozzarella into small

cubes of about ½ inch/1 cm. Cut the ham into equal matchstick-sized lengths.

Spread the tomatoes over the surface of the pizza dough and arrange the rounds of courgette around the outside edge, slightly overlapping each other. Then make a circle of Mozzarella, followed by the ham. Place a few young fennel leaves on the ham. Pour over a trickle of olive oil and sprinkle with the grated Pecorino cheese. Bake in the oven for about 15 minutes.

Meanwhile heat a frying pan with 2 tablespoons of olive oil. Break the egg into a bowl, keeping the yolk intact. When the oil is hot, put in the egg and cook slowly until the white is firm. Cut the egg out with a pastry cutter 4 inches/10 cm in diameter. Sprinkle very lightly with salt and remove from the pan with a flexible spatula. Remove the pizza from the oven and place the egg in the centre. Garnish with more fennel leaves and serve immediately.

Mushroom Pizza
Pizza ai Funghi

To serve 4

12 oz/350 g mushrooms

juice of 1 lemon

olive oil

1 garlic clove

flour

14 oz/400 g bread dough

a little chopped parsley

Preparation and cooking time: 45 minutes

Pre-heat the oven to 400-425°F/ 200-220°C/gas mark 6-7. Peel or wipe the mushrooms and trim the stalks. As they are ready, put them in a bowl of cold water to which the lemon juice has been added. Heat 3 tablespoons of olive oil in a frying pan. Crush the garlic and put it in the hot olive oil. Fry until the garlic browns and then remove from the frying pan. Slice the mushrooms directly into the hot oil and sauté for 3-4 minutes, seasoning with salt and pepper.

Flour a pastry-board and roll the dough into a ball, then flatten it out to a round about 12 inches/30 cm in diameter. Lightly oil a baking tray and place the dough on it. With your fingertips press down the dough just inside the edge to give it a bigger crust. Spread the mushrooms over the pizza and pour over a trickle of olive oil. Sprinkle with chopped parsley and place in the oven for about 15 minutes. Serve hot from the oven, cut into quarters.

Farmhouse Pizza with Ham and Cheese
Pizza Rustica con Prosciutto e Formaggio

To serve 8

12 oz/350 g puff pastry

flour

butter

breadcrumbs

4 oz/100 g ham, sliced

1 large firm tomato

2 oz/50 g Mozzarella cheese

a few sprigs fresh parsley

2 large fresh basil leaves

2 eggs

5 tablespoons whipping cream

2 oz/50 g grated Emmental cheese

nutmeg

a pinch of powdered marjoram

Preparation and cooking time: about 1¼ hours plus any defrosting time

Pre-heat the oven to 375°F/190°C/gas mark 5. Defrost the pastry if frozen. Roll it out on a lightly floured pastry-board until it is large enough to line a shallow, buttered 11 x 7 inch/28 x 18 cm pie dish. Prick the pastry with a fork, sprinkle the base with breadcrumbs and then make an even layer of ham.

Now prepare the filling: blanch the tomato in lightly salted boiling water for a few seconds, then immerse it in cold water. Skin, cut in half and remove the seeds. Cut the tomato into irregular pieces. Dice the Mozzarella cheese and finely chop the parsley with the basil. In a bowl, whisk the eggs with the cream, the grated Emmental cheese, salt, pepper and a little grated nutmeg. Add a pinch of marjoram and then put the chopped tomato into the bowl together with the diced Mozzarella and the chopped parsley and basil. Mix well and pour into the pie dish. Bake in the lower part of the oven for about 35 minutes and serve hot from the oven.

Farmhouse pizza

Pizza with Capers
Pizza 'in Fiore'

To serve 4-6

olive oil

1 packet pizza mix

a little flour

4 oz/125 g Mozzarella cheese

1 thick slice ham

24 capers in vinegar

a few fresh basil leaves

Preparation and cooking time: about 40 minutes
Grease a 10-inch/25 cm round baking tray. Pour the pizza mix into a bowl, add the amount of cold water specified and 2 tablespoons of olive oil; knead until you obtain a smooth, elastic dough. Roll out on a lightly floured pastry-board until large enough to cover the bottom and come part-way up the sides of the pan. Spread the tomato from the packet over the dough, salt and sprinkle with any herbs provided.

Pre-heat the oven to the temperature indicated. Slice the Mozzarella cheese and place the slices like wheel spokes on the tomato sauce; cut the slice of ham into little squares and place them with the well-drained capers between the slices of Mozzarella cheese. Pepper lightly and sprinkle with 3-4

tablespoons of olive oil. Cook the pizza in the pre-heated oven for the length of time shown on the packet; then put it on a serving board, garnish with fresh basil leaves and serve immediately.

*Pizza of many flavours (above); **pizza with capers** (below)*

Naples-style Pizza
Pizza alla Napoletana

To serve 1-2

flour

8 oz/250 g pizza dough

olive oil

2-3 fresh or tinned medium tomatoes, skinned

a pinch of oregano

2-3 large fresh basil leaves

1 garlic clove, green shoot removed

Preparation and cooking time: about 30 minutes, plus any defrosting time. Pre-heat the oven to 400-425°F/ 200-220°C/gas mark 6-7. Flour a pastry-board and roll the dough into a ball, then flatten it out to an 8 inch/20 cm round. Lightly grease a baking tray and place the dough on it. With your fingertips, press down the dough just inside the edge to give it a raised edge.

Chop the tomatoes, season with a little salt and a pinch of oregano and spread over the pizza. Wipe the basil leaves with a damp cloth and finely chop them before sprinkling them over the tomato. Finely chop or slice half a garlic clove and sprinkle this on too. Do not spread these ingredients right to the edges of the dough. Drizzle on plenty of good olive oil and bake for about 12 minutes. Serve straight from the oven on a flat, warmed plate.

Pizza of Many Flavours
Pizza Capricciosa

To serve 4

flour

14 oz/400 g pizza dough

8 oz/250 g skinned tomatoes

a pinch of oregano

1 oz/25 g diced Mozzarella cheese

3 fresh basil leaves, chopped

20 fresh mussels

6 artichoke hearts in oil, cut into quarters

6 black olives, stoned and cut into quarters

6 oz/150 g clams

4 oz/100 g baby mushrooms in oil

2 oz/50 g capers

2 thin slices ham, cut into strips

a few slivers Emmental cheese

a little chopped parsley

olive oil

Preparation and cooking time: about 40 minutes plus any defrosting time
Pre-heat the oven to 400-425°F/ 200-230°C/gas mark 6-7. Flour a pastry-board and roll the dough, defrosted if necessary, into a ball, then flatten it out to a 12-inch/30 cm round. Lightly grease a baking tray and place the dough on it. With your fingertips, press down the dough just inside the edge to give it a raised edge. Remove the seeds from the tomatoes and slice finely. Spread over the pizza. Lightly sprinkle with salt and flavour with a pinch of oregano.

Top the pizza in 8 divisions with 8 separate toppings: the Mozzarella cheese sprinkled with the chopped basil, mussels, artichoke hearts, olives, clams, the well-drained mushrooms, the well-drained capers and finally the strips of ham and slivers of Emmental. Sprinkle with the parsley and pour over a trickle of olive oil. Bake for about 15 minutes and serve at once.

Naples-style pizza

Roman-style Pizza
Pizza alla Romana

To serve 1

flour

8 oz/250 g bread or pizza dough

2 fresh medium tomatoes, skinned

3 oz/75 g Mozzarella cheese

a pinch of oregano

3 fresh basil leaves, chopped

2 tablespoons grated Pecorino cheese

olive oil

Preparation and cooking time: 30 minutes plus any defrosting time

Pre-heat the oven to 400-425°F/ 200-220°C/gas mark 6-7. Flour a pastry-board and roll the dough, defrosted if necessary, into a ball, then flatten it out to an 8 inch/20 cm round. Lightly grease a baking tray and place the dough on it. With your fingertips, press down the dough just inside the edge to give it a slightly raised edge.

Remove the seeds from the tomatoes and slice finely. Spread over the pizza. Lightly sprinkle with salt and pepper, a pinch of oregano and the basil. Sprinkle the Pecorino on top and pour over a thin trickle of olive oil. Bake in the oven for 12-14 minutes until the pizza is golden brown. Pour over a thin trickle of oil before serving hot.

Sweetcorn, Ham and Olive Pizza
Schiacciata di Maïs, Prosciutto e Olive

To serve 4

1 small onion, peeled

1½ garlic cloves

olive oil

8 oz/250 g peeled tomatoes

sugar

6 green olives in brine

4 oz/125 g slice of ham

2 oz/50 g rindless Emmental cheese

butter

4 oz/100 g tinned sweetcorn

a pinch of ginger

12 oz/350 g pizza dough

a pinch of oregano

Preparation and cooking time: about 15 minutes plus any defrosting time

Preheat the oven to 400°F/200°C/gas mark 6. Finely slice the onion and garlic clove. Fry in a saucepan with 3 tablespoons of olive oil without browning. Then purée the tomatoes and add them to the pan with a little salt and a pinch of sugar. Mix and simmer gently for about 15 minutes.

Stone and quarter the olives. Cut the ham into short strips. Finely slice the Emmental cheese. Fry the sweetcorn and ½ garlic clove in a large knob of butter for a few seconds and season with a pinch of ginger.

Roll out the dough, defrosted if necessary, into a 10 inch/25 cm round and place on an oiled baking tray. Pour over the tomato sauce and the sweetcorn on top. Arrange the ham, olives and cheese over the pizza and sprinkle with oregano. Pour on a thin trickle of olive oil. Bake for about 15 minutes until golden brown. Transfer to a serving plate or a wooden chopping board and serve immediately, with a seasonal mixed salad.

Roman-style pizza

Sweetcorn, ham and olive pizza *(far right)*

Spicy pasties

Spicy Pasties
Calcioni Piccanti

To serve 4

8 oz/250 g pizza dough

flour

2 oz/50 g Mozzarella cheese

3 oz/75 g mortadella sausage

tomato purée

16 baby mushrooms in oil

a little oregano

a little paprika

1 egg yolk

a little olive oil

Preparation and cooking time: about 45 minutes plus any defrosting time

Pre-heat the oven to 375°F/190°C/ gas mark 5. Roll out the dough, defrosted if necessary, on a floured pastry-board to a thickness of ⅛ inch/3 mm. Cut out 16 circles with a 3 inch/75 mm diameter pastry cutter. Dice the Mozzarella cheese and mortadella sausage finely and place a few cubes in the centre of each of 8 of the dough rounds. Also add a scant teaspoon of tomato purée, 2 well-drained baby mushrooms, a pinch of oregano and a tiny pinch each of paprika and salt. Take care to leave space around the edges.

Brush the edges of each round with egg yolk and cover with the other 8 rounds. Press down firmly to seal in the filling. Grease a baking tray with olive oil and place the pasties on it well apart. Brush the surfaces with egg yolk and cook for 15-20 minutes, until they are golden brown. Remove from the oven and place on a serving dish. Serve at once while they are hot from the oven. They make an excellent first course or snack but can also be served as a light main course.

Piquant Mini-Pizzas
Pizzette Piccanti

To serve 6

6 frozen mini-pizzas 'Margherita'

olive oil

capers in wine vinegar

6 anchovy fillets in oil

12 stuffed green olives

Preparation and cooking time: about 20 minutes

Pre-heat the oven to 400°F/200°C/gas mark 6. Place the mini-pizzas on an oven tray and moisten each one with a little oil, then place them in the oven, still frozen, for 7-8 minutes. In the meantime drain the capers, the anchovies and the olives, and slice the olives into small rounds.

About 2 minutes before the pizzas are ready, when the cheese has melted but not browned, remove them from the oven and place on each one 4-5 capers, 1 fillet of anchovy, and 2 sliced olives. Moisten with a little oil, and put them back in the oven for the last 2 minutes, taking care that they do not brown too much.

Remove the mini-pizzas from the oven and, after arranging them on a serving plate or tray, serve them hot as an hors-d'oeuvre or cut into quarters, with an apéritif.

Artichoke Pasties
Panzarotti di Carciofi

To serve 4

1 lb/500 g pizza dough

6 small artichokes

1 small onion, peeled

½ garlic clove

butter

olive oil

a little chopped parsley

¼ stock cube

4 oz/100 g salami

4 oz/100 g Emmental cheese

oil for frying

Preparation and cooking time: about 1¼ hours

Defrost the dough if necessary. Clean the artichokes, removing the stalks (they can be used for another recipe) and the tips. Remove the outer leaves until you reach the heart. Cut in half and remove the choke using a small corer.

Finely slice the onion and garlic and fry in a large knob of butter and 2 tablespoons of olive oil. Add the artichoke hearts. After a few seconds add the parsley, crumble in the stock cube, add a little pepper and about 6 tablespoons of boiling water. Shake the pan, cover and simmer for 25 minutes, moistening with more boiling water if necessary. The artichokes should be tender and dry in the end. Plunge the pan into cold water to cool.

Cut the salami into 12 sticks, likewise the Emmental cheese. Roll out the pizza dough to ⅛ inch/3-4 mm and from this cut out 12 5-inch/12 cm rounds, kneading and rolling out the trimmings again. On each round of dough place half an artichoke heart, a stick of salami and a stick of Emmental. Then fold the pasty in two and press down the edges to seal.

Heat plenty of oil in a deep-frying pan and when it is hot, fry the pasties a few at a time, until they are brown all over. Remove from the pan with a slotted spoon and drain on kitchen paper. Serve at once.

Calzone with Ricotta
Calzone con la Ricotta

To serve 4-5

12 oz/300 g very fresh Ricotta cheese

3 oz/75 g spicy salami

4 oz/100 g Mozzarella cheese

2 thick slices ham

2 eggs

1 oz/25 g grated Parmesan cheese

1 oz/25 g grated Pecorino cheese

1 lb/500 g pizza dough

olive oil

Preparation and cooking time: about 1 hour

Pre-heat the oven to 400°F/200°C/ gas mark 6. Sieve the Ricotta into a bowl. Cut the salami into small cubes and the Mozzarella cheese into larger cubes. Coarsely chop the ham, then add all these ingredients to the Ricotta. Bind with the 2 whole eggs, the Parmesan and Pecorino cheeses, salt and pepper and mix thoroughly. Taste and, if necessary, adjust the seasoning.

Roll out the bread dough on a lightly floured pastry-board to an 11-12 inch/ 30 cm diameter circle. Place the Ricotta mixture over half the circle to within about ¾ inch/15 mm of the edge. Fold the other half of the dough over the filling, sealing the two edges by pinching them together. Place the calzone on an greased baking tray and brush it with olive oil; put it in the oven for about 25 minutes. Serve.

Calzone with ricotta

Savoury Calzone
Calzone di Tropea

To serve 4

12 oz/350 g red onions, finely sliced

olive oil

12 stoned black olives in brine

2 tablespoons capers

6 anchovy fillets in oil

a small handful of parsley

2 large fresh basil leaves

14 oz/400 g pizza dough

3 tablespoons grated Pecorino cheese

1 tablespoon breadcrumbs

2 tablespoons tomato sauce

Preparation and cooking time: about 1 hour plus any defrosting time

Pre-heat the oven to 400°F/200°C/gas mark 6. Gently fry the onions in 4 tablespoons of olive oil and lightly sprinkle with salt and pepper. Make sure they do not brown. Quarter the olives. Drain the capers and crush the anchovies. Finely chop the parsley and basil together.

Flour a pastry-board and roll the dough, defrosted if necessary, into a ball, then flatten it out to a 16-inch/40 cm round. Lightly grease a baking tray and place the dough on it. With your fingertips, press down the dough just inside the edge to give it a raised edge. Brush half the surface with olive oil and sprinkle with 2 tablespoons of cheese.

Add to the onions, which should have cooled by now, the capers, olives, parsley and basil, anchovies and the breadcrumbs. Mix well. Spread half this mixture on the part of the dough sprinkled with Pecorino to within 1¼ inches/3 cm of the edge. Spoon on the tomato sauce and sprinkle with grated cheese.

Make another 2 layers with the rest of the ingredients (the aromatic mixture and the cheese) and fold the dough over into a semicircle to cover the filling. Seal the edges and bake on a greased baking tray for about 30 minutes. Remove and leave for a few minutes, then serve on a wooden platter.

INDEX